A BETROTHAL

A ONE-ACT PLAY
BY LANFORD WILSON

★

★

DRAMATISTS
PLAY SERVICE
INC.

A BETROTHAL
Copyright © 1986, Lanford Wilson

All Rights Reserved

For Uta Hagen and
Herbert Berghof

SCENE

The corner of a large tent. A flap door nearby. Folding card tab
large coffee urn, paper cups, milk cartons, folding chairs, progr
on some chairs. Drizzle outside.

An afternoon in mid-May.

CHARACTERS

Ms. J.H. Joslyn
Mr. Kermit Wasserman

A BETROTHAL

Ms. J.H. Joslyn enters, miffed. She is perhaps fifty, attractive but doesn't care, maybe a little heavy and doesn't care about that either. She has got herself up in a neat suit and is annoyed that she bothered. She throws off a makeshift plastic bag or some such rain protection.

JOSLYN. But then, what did I expect? What could I possibly have expected? *(Pours coffee from the urn, without skipping a beat she shakes three milk cartons, they are empty, pours the dribble from two into the one, pours a bit of coffee in the one, sloshes it about, pours milk into cup.)* I expected nothing. *(Sits, sips.)* I had no expectations. The bastards. It's the way of the world; it's the lay of the land. Well, if they have not eyes in their heads! If they're blind to progress. Pearls before swine. What did I expect? *(Looking off.)* Haven't got sense enough to come in out of the rain. Pouring on them; ruining the whole show. Good. Fogging up their bi-focals. Not that they could see anyway: *(Mimicing.)* "Oh, my, isn't that quaint. Oh, how cunning; fetching color, delightful rhythm; amusing play of the various parts. A bit coarse, of course." What faggots. Well, what did I expect? I said there was no hope. I had no hope. The situation was clear from the beginning. It was a hopeless situation. What did I expect? *(Mr. Wasserman enters. Dejected. Sighs. He is perhaps sixty, neat, and though he is a large man he is decidedly soft, almost delicate. Looks around, seeing nothing. Shakes water from his umbrella, stands it somewhere. Murmurs: "Oh, my..." Pours coffee. Sits on the other side of the table.)* There's no milk.
WASSERMAN. No, fine, thank you, nothing serious...
JOSLYN. I took the last.
WASSERMAN. I'm sorry?
JOSLYN. Of the milk.

5

WASSERMAN. Oh. No, no, I ... just needed to hold something.
I'll be fine. *(Pause.)* Oh, dear...

JOSLYN. They're getting soaked.

WASSERMAN. Yes, they'll like that. That's something.

JOSLYN. The people. Haven't got the sense to come in out of the
rain.

WASSERMAN. No, it's stopped. Nearly. Nearly stopped.
They're all but finished, anyway. They finished the Tall Beardeds
before it started, so no damage done ... They're on the Arils,
now.

JOSLYN. Damn the Arils. Shouldn't even be in the show.

WASSERMAN. No, not my thing, though interesting, I suppose
... to those who ... find them interesting.

JOSLYN. Too damn particular.

WASSERMAN. Yes, very fussy I'm told.

JOSLYN. Ship 'em back to Persia or wherever the hell they came
from. Don't belong here.

WASSERMAN. I've had no first hand experience with them, I'm
sure they're very rewarding ... to those who ... find them very
rewarding.

JOSLYN. Waste of energy.

WASSERMAN. Oh, I'm sure.

JOSLYN. Look like shit, anyway.

WASSERMAN. They are terribly muddy, some of them, for
my taste.

JOSLYN. Fuck 'em.

WASSERMAN. *(Starts.)* Ah, when I was leaving the house, and
of course, it was so early, I had this terrible feeling that I was miss-
ing something — couldn't for the life of me — that's always so
annoying — then, of course, half-way here, in the middle of the
Parkway, I realized I'd forgotten my galoshes. I had to pull over, I
can't think and drive; it certainly looked like rain. I'd remembered
my raincoat, my... of course I was so nervous because this is my first
time.

JOSLYN. *(Beat.)* What are you talking about?

WASSERMAN. To show. So I didn't want to be late. So of course it did. Rain. I mean, I didn't go back so of course ... it ... I don't mind ruining my shoes so much, but I hope I don't come down with something. Of course it's probably just nerves It did rain very hard there for a moment.

JOSLYN. I hope it ruins everything.

WASSERMAN. I come every year, but this is the first time I've had the nerve to show. Actually the first time I thought I had something really very special Vanity. Oh, dear, dear...

JOSLYN. You're a breeder.

WASSERMAN. Yes, and you?

JOSLYN. Ummm. Pearls before swine. I thought you were a judge. You have that judgy look.

WASSERMAN. Oh, no, no, I wouldn't presume.

JOSLYN. Your first?

WASSERMAN. Uh, yes, and, uh, never again. At least not for years. I haven't the strength. I should have known. Hubris. Ah, well. Oh, dear ... poor little darling. Such a sweetheart. Never should have exposed her to the harsh ... light ... of reality ... in the world ... of the real. And me. Oh, dear.

JOSLYN. You might as well know I have no use for you or any of your kind.

WASSERMAN. I'm sorry?

JOSLYN. Vulgar, disgusting, tasteless, showy and useless in a garden. So expect no sympathy.

WASSERMAN. Then, what are you doing here?

JOSLYN. *(She keeps her cards very close to her chest.)* I have my own pursuits, thank you, I've been scoffed at before. I'm quite immune. Slings and arrows; roll right off my back.

WASSERMAN. I understood you were a breeder, too.

JOSLYN. I have my pursuits. Nothing you would understand. For your information I was tickled pink when it started to rain. The spectacle of that huge, vulgar mess of a Tall Bearded that they had just awarded Best of Show, falling right over flat in the mud the moment they turned their backs! Ha! Everyone running to stake it up. In five minutes the whole damn lot of them were leaning and staggering like drunken sailors. No wind, mind you, just a spring shower. And my baby was standing up at attention like a little soldier.

WASSERMAN. Which one is your Little Soldier?

JOSLYN. I have my pursuits.

WASSERMAN. I really must say. *(Looking around.)* I have no love for the Tall Beardeds. I'm an Intermediate Breeder. May I take it you're an Intermediate Breeder, too?

JOSLYN. I have my pursuits.

WASSERMAN. I'm so glad, I never really go to any of the meetings, I couldn't possibly. I get the Quarterly, I pour over the Quarterly ... uh ... which one is your Little Soldier?

JOSLYN. Never you mind, never you mind. Slings and arrows. I came back to the tent because I thought no one would be here. Everyone was acres away down at the other end, I expected to be alone here.

WASSERMAN. Yes, it did look very deserted.

JOSLYN. It was, then you came.

WASSERMAN. Yes, yes, I simply couldn't any longer. I was trying to be brave, but I came all over with the feeling I was going to faint. I simply had to sit down. Little Tanya stood up to the rain at first, she just sparkled like dew, but I'm certain she was beginning to feel it. I gave her a little shake, I don't think anyone saw. As soon as I looked around I realized I'd been wrong to enter Big Judy, I told her I was sorry, but for Little Tanya — to be overlooked — I know, of course, she's frail. Part of her charm for me. Oh, such vanity. Never again.

JOSLYN. I have no idea whom you're talking about.

WASSERMAN. Oh, I'm sorry. I thought...

JOSLYN. Who are these women? Why are you telling me about them? I don't know them. I don't know anyone. I wouldn't like them. I want to be alone here.

WASSERMAN. Oh, no, they're my babies, of course. They're in the trial garden of the Intermediate Iris Bed. I thought Little Tanya had a very good chance of attracting attention.

JOSLYN. You named your iris Big Judy and Little Tanya?

WASSERMAN. Maybe you at least noticed Tanya. Many people

seemed attracted to her — but, alas ... not ... oh, dear...

JOSLYN. I noticed nothing. I don't parade about ooing and ahing, thank you. I guarded my entry. I wouldn't put it past some of these — I saw their jealous eyes, their itchy fingers. I stood my ground.

WASSERMAN. Over your Little Soldier? I saw everything. I must say I thought some were very inferior. Others, frankly, I know what you mean, made me not jealous at all, but simply burn with envy. I do think the Intermediates are just developing in leaps and ... such strong branching, what texture.

JOSLYN. Branching. You know nothing of branching; nothing of texture.

WASSERMAN. It's just that it's something I've neglected horribly. Something I must take the time to work on.

JOSLYN. Time, oh, time. Try thirty years.

WASSERMAN. I'm sorry?

JOSLYN. Of no other thought. Day and night. Try perfection.

WASSERMAN. That's remarkable.

JOSLYN. Ha. Tell it to the judge.

WASSERMAN. Oh, dear. Oh, your Little Soldier wasn't overlooked?

JOSLYN. I expected nothing.

WASSERMAN. Oh, I must say I was foolish enough to expect Best of Show.

JOSLYN. I had no expectations.

WASSERMAN. Oh, I so hoped.

JOSLYN. I had no hope. What did I expect? Another story of the unsung hero. Slaving in their labs; Marie Curie in that godawful unheated barn, day and night. All the nameless laborers of the field. Who knows their plight? Who their hopes and dreams? Who celebrates their tiny joys? The doubling of chromosomes, the increase of bud-count. The miracle of texture. Perfectly round falls that stand out utterly horizontally in a hurricane! Triple branching, and at ninety degrees not a hundred eighty, who's ever seen it before? Who will ever know who changed the course of history? Who will care? Lost in the shuffle. Taken for granted. The builder of the

9

Trojan Horse, the inventor of the wheel, the discoverer of Pluto, the principle of pi... What in the hell are you doing? *(He has been searching through a pocket notebook.)*

WASSERMAN. I have it here — "Good blue," no, "Bad yellow," branching, branching, texture ... somewhere ... "Lovely white," no ... AH! you are *(Reading.)* J.H. Joslyn, Carmel, New York. And your Little Soldier is entry number 3a-I-916.

JOSLYN. What have you got there?

WASSERMAN. I take copious notes. "Most outstanding falls, utterly round, perfectly horizontal, astonishing branching, holding flowers quite apart, remarkable texture of fall and standard, terribly unfortunate muddiness in —" and so on, and so on. I must say, Ms., er, ah, Joslyn, I'm very pleased to meet the breeder of that Little Soldier. I made special note of Carmel, as I'm from Mahopac, which is a hop skip and a jump down the road.

JOSLYN. Were I from Carmel, I'd certainly know the whereabouts of a town so nearby and visibly disagreeable as Mahopac.

WASSERMAN. I must say I can't believe your Little Soldier didn't at least receive a citation for extraordinary branching and texture. Why, the branches are at angles to one another instead of directly across from — I must say, what dimension it gives the whole stalk. Like a candelabra; I've never seen it before.

JOSLYN. Neither has anyone. Nor do they care, apparently. The builder of the Great Wall of China, the—

WASSERMAN. And texture! Like carved ivory. I actually reached to feel the thickness — quite inadvertently, I didn't even realize I'd done it — the way one instinctively smells a rose.

JOSLYN. I know nothing of smelling roses. I have no use for them. Or for what you call instinct, which of course is thoughtlessness.

WASSERMAN. I didn't feel it, however. Someone barked at me so fiercely I just moved on, but I certainly took note. You're starred in my book, and there are only four of five entries that are starred.

JOSLYN. Humf!

10

WASSERMAN. I'm sorry?

JOSLYN. What care I? Slings and arrows. One among four, one among five, right off my back.

WASSERMAN. I'm sorry?

JOSLYN. *(Looking at him levelly.)* Oh, yes. Humf! Oh, sure ... I've seen you.

WASSERMAN. Oh, well, there you have the advantage, I'm afraid ... I ... maybe it's unsocial, but I ... at a flower show, at least ... I don't think I see people. I'm taking notes, moving on, admiring, getting so many ideas, that I think perhaps I don't look ... uh ... up. And then, of course, I find it so confusing to look at people. What if I should catch their eye? A perfect stranger? What would they think? And maybe it would be a judge, thinking I was trying to influence him ... or ... her ... in some influential way.

JOSLYN. At the Grand Union. On Route Six.

WASSERMAN. I'm sorry?

JOSLYN. Pawing the lettuce and teasing the kiwi fruit. It's only a bad habit, you know, neglectful mother, probably. Father away at sea a good deal, or some such. It could be corrected with a little self-discipline.

WASSERMAN. I'm sorry?

JOSLYN. Pinching, testing, squeezing, pawing. Some people think they're the only man on God's Earth. Mauling everything, trying to make it their own. How would you feel if you were the iris? How would you feel if you were the fruit?

WASSERMAN. I'm sorry?

JOSLYN. It can be corrected.

WASSERMAN. What's that?

JOSLYN. A word to the wise...

WASSERMAN. *(Reaching out his hand.)* You must admit the texture of your Little Soldier's falls invites the touch. It looks like it would feel of .... oooo, I don't know of velvet or chamois or ivory or oooo, something extraordinary.

JOSLYN. *(Slapping his hand.)* Just never you mind, sir. Never you worry about it. You're not the only one, remember.

WASSERMAN. I'm sorry?

JOSLYN. Reaching out their grubby paws to cop a feel. There was fifty if there was one. Two judges, if you believe it. With their judgy little thumb and finger. I put them in their places, don't think I didn't. Inadequate guidance at school probably. All this permissive behavior.

WASSERMAN. Thirty years ... my goodness. I've been working that long of course, but I would never presume, I wouldn't know where to begin. I breed for color, so I wouldn't know—

JOSLYN. Color, oh, my goodness! Yappidy-yap, yappidy-yap, it's all I hear. Blue this and puce that. Ruby Glow and Pink Reward.

WASSERMAN. Oh, when I first saw my first Lillipinkput, I began to work the very next week.

JOSLYN. Sing me no first Lillipinkputs, read me no rhymes, thank you. It's all I hear. One has enough to contend with without your Lillipinkputs.

WASSERMAN. I was quite inspired by her. I saw a whole clump blooming in Presby Gardens, before she won the Sass Award, and I must say I was bowled over by her.

JOSLYN. Sing me no Sass Awards, read me no bowled overs, I've no use for it at all.

WASSERMAN. Your world, of course, is of quite a different order.

JOSLYN. I have my pursuits.

WASSERMAN. You wouldn't see it, I quite realize.

JOSLYN. I'm not blind. I could be impressed. I can see, and what I see is as far as any of them have gone. There's one today, hardly to be overlooked, tangerine, maybe, orange maybe, I have eyes. Striking color, but then what? I went over to it, one could hardly fail to see it, but on close inspection — the hypocrisy! Flimsy wouldn't begin. Insubstantial, wilting falls lying practically flat against the sheating spathe, crest styles of crepe paper, standards so tissue thin I'm surprised the first drop of rain didn't go straight through them. One branch, mind you, and it hardly held up even this aenemic, cobwebby—

WASSERMAN. *(Hardly audible.)* Madam.

12

JOSLYN. — pissant of a — and God knows the bud count. Probably not even two. Nothing so wispy could—
WASSERMAN. Madam.
JOSLYN. — support more. And a crowd around it ooing and ahing! Over this feeble, —
WASSERMAN. Madam.
JOSLYN. — debilitated, sapless, pithless, impotent, —
WASSERMAN. *(A little louder.)* Madam.
JOSLYN. — Lustless, flaccid, feckless, limp —
WASSERMAN. Madam!
JOSLYN. Wishy-washy, insipid — !
WASSERMAN. *(Quite huge.)* MADAM, YOU ARE SPEAKING OF MY CHILD!
JOSLYN. *(Beat.)* I beg your pardon?
WASSERMAN. *(Still outraged.)* You are speaking of Little Tanya! Though she may not be to your liking, many people were very admiring. Several times when I drew close enough to hear their remarks, several people were wondering if the breeder was at the show. Many were struck. *(His hand on his throat.)* I think I've injured my voice. I'm terribly sorry. I don't know what I can be thinking. I've never spoken like that before to anyone. Once to a very, *very* truculent raspberry, never to a person. Certainly not a lady. It's the strain of the occasion. I've not been myself all day. I shouldn't be around people, they make me terribly ... and the agony of competition, it isn't human. Oh, dear...
JOSLYN. *(After a beat.)* That *vapidity* is Little Tanya?
WASSERMAN. *(Eyes closed, a strangled admission.)* Yes...
JOSLYN. That *whisper?*
WASSERMAN. Please. I know she isn't to your taste.
JOSLYN. I say nothing of my taste.
WASSERMAN. I realize you're working in quite a different field.
JOSLYN. Fields abound, I say nothing of fields.
WASSERMAN. You have your pursuits.
JOSLYN. Just never you mind.
WASSERMAN. But you must understand another choosing to

13

endeavor in an endeavor of ... another choosing.

JOSLYN. I say nothing of my understanding.

WASSERMAN. That orange has been the achievement of thirty years. And I can't help the vanity of being somewhat ... vain ... about ... achieving it. You understand, failings apart, it is a remarkable orange.

JOSLYN. It's a very good color, as colors come and go.

WASSERMAN. No rose has an orange like it.

JOSLYN. I know nothing of roses.

WASSERMAN. Well, I can tell you any orange rose is impossible to use with anything. Little Tanya is the only orange I've seen, and many people remarked on it, that mixes. She's a mixer! She looks charming with other oranges, with lemons, with peaches, with red. Red! With lavender and blue. She blends! People would want her. Many said so. They can use her. She's a blender!

JOSLYN. I care nothing about what people can use.

WASSERMAN. Well, you should. Many people were remarking about your Little Soldier, you surely heard them...

JOSLYN. Yammerings of the crowd.

WASSERMAN. But it can't be used in a ... what I mean to say is ... it's absolutely... nothing could ... well, exactly what color would you call it? I mean it isn't a light yellow, it isn't buff. It isn't green, it's muddy, sure, but what? mustard? Bluish maybe, but I was at a loss to make out what....

JOSLYN. *(She has been collecting her things and rises.)* I see it's quite impossible to hope that you'll ever leave here. Some people are like that. It's a lack of respect for another's privacy. It's a bad habit, of course, it could be worked on, but in your case I doubt any serious improvement. The rain has let up, I'll remove myself and allow you, doubtless, to find another victim.

WASSERMAN. *(Looking at her with amazement.)* I know you. How extraordinary. I don't know anyone. I've seen you.

JOSLYN. Sing me none of your seens.

WASSERMAN. You're a teacher.

JOSLYN. I beg your pardon, I am not.

WASSERMAN. You most certainly are.

JOSLYN. I am not, I know what I am.

WASSERMAN. You teach.

JOSLYN. I do not.

WASSERMAN. You did, you must have.

JOSLYN. *(Beat.)* I have my pursuits, thank you. What I do and what I've done are not for the ears of idle strangers.

WASSERMAN. Last year you taught!

JOSLYN. I did not!

WASSERMAN. You came to the gate!

JOSLYN. I came to no gate of yours, you can be sure. I peer through no gates, thank you.

WASSERMAN. You came just inside, and there you stood. Looking just as you do now.

JOSLYN. I did not. I come in gates only when I'm invited in, and I'm invited in only where I ask to be and I did not ask, thank you.

WASSERMAN. You came to Castle Crampton. I saw you at the gate. Believe me, I certainly didn't intend to see you, I don't see any of them, they sometimes see me, it can't be helped, they ask their questions, they talk on and on, some of them, it's all very ... and the children pour in on their field trips, the musicians, you know they have hundreds of them for the chamber orchestras, the quartets, and they're so talky, I'm afraid. You were a chaperon to one of the children's classes.

JOSLYN. I beg your pardon, I have no class.

WASSERMAN. And in they poured and there you stood. Just inside the gate.

JOSLYN. In the line of one's employment one is sometimes called upon, quite against one's will to fulfill the place of those who are irresponsible enough to become ill.

WASSERMAN. I would never insist, of course, you know where you did and didn't go. I must say I don't at all feel comfortable around children. They don't seem to watch where they're going, they tend to step on me. But if you're the principal and went along in place of one of the—

JOSLYN. I am certainly not a principal.

15

WASSERMAN. Or an assistant principal with the duty of replacing some—

JOSLYN. I am certainly no assistant principal.

WASSERMAN. Or the librarian and were asked to fill-in for—

JOSLYN. I am not a librarian for any of your—

WASSERMAN. Or the assistant librarian.

JOSLYN. I have my pursuits. You, of course, might be interested in the likes of Castle Crampton Gardens, I assure you I would not be.

WASSERMAN. Oh, my goodness, no.

JOSLYN. I disdained to step one foot into such a place. One look was all I needed to understand the whole of Castle Crampton completely. Tacky little bedded-out beds, looking as though they belonged in front of a gas station.

WASSERMAN. *(Loving it.)* Oh, my goodness!

JOSLYN. Municipal gardening, indeed. Worse here than abroad if you can believe it, and Crampton worst of all.

WASSERMAN. Oh, yes!

JOSLYN. I know the philosophy. Rows of wax begonias, never was a plant so aptly named, your cup of tea, well, you can have it. No doubt Little Tanya would blend in well...

WASSERMAN. Oh, dear, no. I'm afraid even Tanya couldn't save the place.

JOSLYN. All your geometrical beds, squares and circles and triangles. Yellow marigolds, surrounded by a cunning little ring of blue Ageratum houstonianum, surrounded by a nice contrasting lipstick red of, maybe, Salvia Splendens "Harbinger." "Castle Crampton" spelled out in Petunias and Lobelia. They might as well use spray paint. A Spanish castle, A Venetian court, a ballroom lawn, no doubt, with German statuary.

WASSERMAN. Yes, yes, yes ... all of it.

JOSLYN. Tulips by the hundreds, I'm sure, in the spring.

WASSERMAN. By the thousands! I plant them, they buy them by the truckloads, ripped out the day they're shot and replaced by marigolds, not even stock.

JOSLYN. You plant them? You? Not just an innocent tourist, but responsible for that mess?

WASSERMAN. Oh, Lord no, responsible, never, I wouldn't presume. I wouldn't make a decision myself, what if someone saw it? Oh, I'm terribly sorry, I know you and you don't know me, what am I thinking ... I'm not in the habit of meeting ... allow me to introduce ... uh, Ms. J.H. Joslyn, this is Mr. Kermit Wasserman; Mr. Wasserman, Ms. Joslyn. How do you do? It is my misfortune to be one of the assistant gardeners at Crampton.

JOSLYN. How do you do? I was just going.

WASSERMAN. Oh, my yes, I'm afraid you'd better, because if you're going to be wicked about Crampton, I couldn't tear myself away and I shouldn't hear it. My own garden, of course, very small, is a cottagy, Englishy sort of thing, very modest, but enough for me and my iris. And yours?

JOSLYN. Sing me no yourses, my garden's my garden. Certainly not Englishy cottagy. I farm, I don't decorate. I breed. I grow eggplant and squash, kale and kohlrabi. And I breed intermediate iris for strength and substance. I'm none of your watercolorists.

WASSERMAN. You're not, by any chance, colorblind?

JOSLYN. I beg your pardon?

WASSERMAN. I'm terribly sorry, I don't know what came over me. It's just that one who has created such a lovely texture and, as you say, substance, and neglected so completely—

JOSLYN. Rolls right off my back. There's no reason for me to stay, what did I expect? I don't know how some people call themselves scientists.

WASSERMAN. Ms. Joslyn, I may be vain, I may have expected too much, but you cannot—

JOSLYN. How could you have overlooked so basic a thing as stalk?

WASSERMAN. I could say the same for you, you know, were I the sort who—

JOSLYN. The color may be striking but there's nothing under it!

WASSERMAN. You have created a castle without a flag!

JOSLYN. I care for more than flashy headgear, thank you!

WASSERMAN. And you might as well be breeding galoshes!

JOSLYN. I am a great breeder, sir!

WASSERMAN. And, madam, so am I!

JOSLYN. I've toiled in the fields, sir, for thirty years!

WASSERMAN. And so have I!

JOSLYN. And you've nothing to show for it.

WASSERMAN. No one wants your Little Soldier!

JOSLYN. No on needs your Tanya!

WASSERMAN. If my Tanya had the texture of your Little Soldier!

JOSLYN. If my Soldier had the color of Tanya...! *(There is a dead pause. It extends. Their words hang in the air. They think for a moment. They consider, each with their own thoughts. They picture it. She sits.)*

WASSERMAN. *(Imagining it.)* Oh, my ...

JOSLYN. Hummm ...

WASSERMAN. Oh, my, that would be something ...

JOSLYN. Hummmmm ...

WASSERMAN. In four years ... maybe five. Six at the outside... Can you see it?

JOSLYN. *(Musing.)* Just never mind, I see what I see...

WASSERMAN. I've never seen anything like it.

JOSLYN. There's never been anything like it.

WASSERMAN. Not to push, and I don't think it's vanity, but Best of Show would be in the bag.

JOSLYN. In a jerkwater show like this? I wouldn't waste our time.

WASSERMAN. One might easily interest the nurseries in such a ... uh...

JOSLYN. Oh, my good man, beating them away with our umbrellas.

WASSERMAN. The Sass Award is not at all out of the question.

JOSLYN. Sing me no Sass Awards, we're talking the cover of the Royal Horticultural Society's Garden Magazine.

WASSERMAN. Perhaps you had better be listed as breeder, I wouldn't be able to tolerate the limelight. Fame has always...

JOSLYN. *(Musing.)* Sing me no limelight, read me no fame; we're talking fortune.

WASSERMAN. Indeed. Not to be crass, but...?

JOSLYN. Thousands. Tens of thousands.

WASSERMAN. A better income, I would think than assisting at a school library.

JOSLYN. Fuck the school library.

WASSERMAN. Indeed.

JOSLYN. Fuck Castle Crampton.

WASSERMAN. Oh, indeed. *(A long pause, they dream. Then delicately turn to particulars. She clears her throat.)*

JOSLYN. *(Inquiring lightly.)* Ah ... how are .. her ... uh ... rhizomes?

WASSERMAN. Well, actually, now that you ask, very strong indeed, really quite remarkable.

JOSLYN. Are they?

WASSERMAN. And ... uh ... his?

JOSLYN. Well, uh ... adequate certainly ... uh ... perhaps not absolutely ... the ... uh...

WASSERMAN. Only that?

JOSLYN. I've probably seen better increase.

WASSERMAN. Tanya increases like a weed.

JOSLYN. *Does* she? The little devil.

WASSERMAN. And, uh, his ... seed pod?

JOSLYN. Oh, marvelous, of course, with all that upper strength. Unfailing.

WASSERMAN. I thought so. I must tell you, Tanya has been known to disappoint me there.

JOSLYN. Well, she's terribly delicate, it would be uncaring to expect..

WASSERMAN. I'm afraid, though, we'd much better have your Little Soldier as the seed parent.

JOSLYN. Absolutely. He won't mind playing the girl. Not for Little Tanya. Of the Golden Hair! I assume the bud-count, actually...?

19

WASSERMAN. Oh, yes, two. And she has been known to have two branches.

JOSLYN. Oh, I'm glad to hear it. That might make it much easier. Though we have to get some starch in her. Strengthen those limbs. Not stout — just strong. He'll do wonders for that.

WASSERMAN. And as for color, I'm glad to say, there, Tanya is very dominant.

JOSLYN. The little vixen! He's not very sure of himself there, I'm glad to say.

WASSERMAN. Oh, she'll take care of him nicely.

JOSLYN. My, my, my....

WASSERMAN. I must say...

JOSLYN. So convenient that you live so close.

WASSERMAN. Isn't it?

JOSLYN. Lovely Mahopac. *(Pause.)* You understand, I think this should be exclusive. I don't want to see her red hair pussy-footing around with—

WASSERMAN. Madam! You overreach yourselef. Tanya's fidelity, I assure you is irreproachable. You had much better be concerned about your Little Soldier.

JOSLYN. You have his word.

WASSERMAN. Well ... one hears stories...

JOSLYN. Would you agree to begin with my seed bed? I make all my own soil, pure compost. A good grade of builders sand.

WASSERMAN. That's quite fine by me ... You won't mind if I visit the site first, just to ...

JOSLYN. Oh, by all means. I think we should begin first thing in the morning. I'll drive over to your place...

WASSERMAN. Oh, excellent, excellent ... We can collect her lovely pollen at the crack of dawn...

JOSLYN. I have a divine set of sable brushes — never been touched. So exorbitant, but I couldn't help myself.

WASSERMAN. How impulsive!

JOSLYN. Oh, I know. I've been waiting for the right occasion... I knew it'd come.

WASSERMAN. Intuition... I don't expect to sleep a wink.

JOSLYN. Nor I.

WASSERMAN. Well I must say. *(He gets up, walks a few steps, a new dignity.)* They're all drifting back, the judging must be over. Ha! If they only knew.

JOSLYN. Look at them. Do you watch the presentation of the ribbons? And all their giggling little squeals when they win?

WASSERMAN. Not usually, I'm afraid. Crowds, you know, with nothing to look at ... except people, of course ... but perhaps this year ... just to see how it's done. Just to get into practice.

JOSLYN. Might as well get in the habit of being notable. I must say, Mr. Wasserman, you're looking like a championship breeder.

WASSERMAN. And you, Ms. Joslyn.

JOSLYN. Ah! The sun's come out. And look who's golden hair is flashing in the light. She must be a hundred yards away.

WASSERMAN. She has reason to be excited tonight.

JOSLYN. I'm as nervous as a schoolgirl

WASSERMAN. I think you're blushing.

JOSLYN. So are you.

WASSERMAN. Well, let us sit here, then, and wait for the onslaught of the unsuspecting crowd. *(They sit.)*

JOSLYN. I must say it has been a very good show this year. *(They open their programs and begin to study them.)*

CURTAIN

PROPERTIES

ON STAGE
Folding card table
Large coffee urn
Paper cups
Milk cartons (mostly empty)
Folding chairs
Flower show programs, on some chairs

OFF STAGE
Plastic bag, used as rain shield (Joslyn)
Pocket notebook (Wasserman)

NEW PLAYS

★ **I'LL EAT YOU LAST: A CHAT WITH SUE MENGERS by John Logan.** For more than 20 years, Sue Mengers' clients were the biggest names in show business: Barbra Streisand, Faye Dunaway, Burt Reynolds, Ali MacGraw, Gene Hackman, Cher, Candice Bergen, Ryan O'Neal, Nick Nolte, Mike Nichols, Gore Vidal, Bob Fosse…If her clients were the talk of the town, she was the town, and her dinner parties were the envy of Hollywood. Now, you're invited into her glamorous Beverly Hills home for an evening of dish, dirty secrets and all the inside showbiz details only Sue can tell you. "A delectable soufflé of a solo show…thanks to the buoyant, witty writing of Mr. Logan" –NY Times. "80 irresistible minutes of primo tinseltown dish from a certified master chef." –Hollywood Reporter. [1W] ISBN: 978-0-8222-3079-3

★ **PUNK ROCK by Simon Stephens.** In a private school outside of Manchester, England, a group of highly-articulate seventeen-year-olds flirt and posture their way through the day while preparing for their A-Level mock exams. With hormones raging and minimal adult supervision, the students must prepare for their future — and survive the savagery of high school. Inspired by playwright Simon Stephens' own experiences as a teacher, PUNK ROCK is an honest and unnerving chronicle of contemporary adolescence. "[A] tender, ferocious and frightning play." –NY Times. "[A] muscular little play that starts out funny and ferocious then reveals its compassion by degrees." –Hollywood Reporter. [5M, 3W] ISBN: 978-0-8222-3288-9

★ **THE COUNTRY HOUSE by Donald Margulies.** A brood of famous and longing-to-be-famous creative artists have gathered at their summer home during the Williamstown Theatre Festival. When the weekend takes an unexpected turn, everyone is forced to improvise, inciting a series of simmering jealousies, romantic outbursts, and passionate soul-searching. Both witty and compelling, THE COUNTRY HOUSE provides a piercing look at a family of performers coming to terms with the roles they play in each other's lives. "A valentine to the artists of the stage." –NY Times. "Remarkably candid and funny." –Variety. [3M, 3W] ISBN: 978-0-8222-3274-2

★ **OUR LADY OF KIBEHO by Katori Hall.** Based on real events, OUR LADY OF KIBEHO is an exploration of faith, doubt, and the power and consequences of both. In 1981, a village girl in Rwanda claims to see the Virgin Mary. Ostracized by her schoolmates and labeled disturbed, everyone refuses to believe, until impossible happenings appear again and again. Skepticism gives way to fear, and then to belief, causing upheaval in the school community and beyond. "Transfixing." –NY Times. "Hall's passionate play renews belief in what theater can do." –Time Out [7M, 8W, 1 boy] ISBN: 978-0-8222-3301-5

DRAMATISTS PLAY SERVICE, INC.
440 Park Avenue South, New York, NY 10016 212-683-8960 Fax 212-213-1539
postmaster@dramatists.com www.dramatists.com

NEW PLAYS

★ **AGES OF THE MOON by Sam Shepard.** Byron and Ames are old friends, reunited by mutual desperation. Over bourbon on ice, they sit, reflect and bicker until fifty years of love, friendship and rivalry are put to the test at the barrel of a gun. "A poignant and honest continuation of themes that have always been present in the work of one of this country's most important dramatists, here reconsidered in the light and shadow of time passed." –NY Times. "Finely wrought…as enjoyable and enlightening as a night spent stargazing." –Talkin' Broadway. [2M] ISBN: 978-0-8222-2462-4

★ **ALL THE WAY by Robert Schenkkan. Winner of the 2014 Tony Award for Best Play.** November, 1963. An assassin's bullet catapults Lyndon Baines Johnson into the presidency. A Shakespearean figure of towering ambition and appetite, this charismatic, conflicted Texan hurls himself into the passage of the Civil Rights Act—a tinderbox issue emblematic of a divided America—even as he campaigns for re-election in his own right, and the recognition he so desperately wants. In Pulitzer Prize and Tony Award–winning Robert Schenkkan's vivid dramatization of LBJ's first year in office, means versus ends plays out on the precipice of modern America. ALL THE WAY is a searing, enthralling exploration of the morality of power. It's not personal, it's just politics. "…action-packed, thoroughly gripping… jaw-dropping political drama." –Variety. "A theatrical coup…nonstop action. The suspense of a first-class thriller." –NY1. [17M, 3W] ISBN: 978-0-8222-3181-3

★ **CHOIR BOY by Tarell Alvin McCraney.** The Charles R. Drew Prep School for Boys is dedicated to the creation of strong, ethical black men. Pharus wants nothing more than to take his rightful place as leader of the school's legendary gospel choir. Can he find his way inside the hallowed halls of this institution if he sings in his own key? "[An] affecting and honest portrait…of a gay youth tentatively beginning to find the courage to let the truth about himself become known." –NY Times. "In his stirring and stylishly told drama, Tarell Alvin McCraney cannily explores race and sexuality and the graces and gravity of history." –NY Daily News. [7M] ISBN: 978-0-8222-3116-5

★ **THE ELECTRIC BABY by Stefanie Zadravec.** When Helen causes a car accident that kills a young man, a group of fractured souls cross paths and connect around a mysterious dying baby who glows like the moon. Folk tales and folklore weave throughout this magical story of sad endings, strange beginnings and the unlikely people that get you from one place to the next. "The imperceptible magic that pervades human existence and the power of myth to assuage sorrow are invoked by the playwright as she entwines the lives of strangers in THE ELECTRIC BABY, a touching drama." –NY Times. "As dazzling as the dialogue is dreamful." –Pittsburgh City Paper. [3M, 3W] ISBN: 978-0-8222-3011-3

DRAMATISTS PLAY SERVICE, INC.
440 Park Avenue South, New York, NY 10016 212-683-8960 Fax 212-213-1539
postmaster@dramatists.com www.dramatists.com

It was only the t

testing, but none of Jean-Luc's friends were left. . . .

The room was made of perfectly black ... outlined by the gold line of holoconductors. Jean-Luc Pica... om-man...

Th... n.

H... a cram... for-ward... his ship...

"C...

"... *de Leon*...

Je... that ship... he knew... inst in th...

In... into two Romulan destroyers. What resulted was less a fight than an act of annihilation. The *Ponce de Leon* had been lost with all hands.

"This simulation will begin in fifteen seconds."

Star Trek: The Next Generation
STARFLEET ACADEMY

Star Trek: Deep Space Nine

Star Trek movie tie-in

Star Trek Generations

Available from MINSTREL Books

STARFLEET ACADEMY™ #8

STARFALL

Brad and
Barbara Strickland

Interior illustrations by
Todd Cameron Hamilton

A MINSTREL®
BOOK

Published by POCKET BOOKS
New York   London   Toronto   Sydney   Tokyo   Singapore

A MINSTREL PAPERBACK *Original*

A Minstrel Book published by
POCKET BOOKS, a division of Simon & Schuster Inc.
1230 Avenue of the Americas, New York, NY 10020

STAR TREK is a Registered Trademark of
Paramount Pictures

This book is published by Pocket Books, a division of
Simon & Schuster Inc., under exclusive license from
Paramount Pictures.

ISBN: 0-671-51010-X

First Minstrel Books printing October 1995

10 9 8 7 6 5 4 3 2 1

A MINSTREL BOOK and colophon are registered trademarks
of Simon & Schuster Inc.

Cover art by Catherine Huerta

Printed in the U.S.A.

For Dorothy, Sheila,
and especially David

STARFLEET TIMELINE

2264

The launch of Captain James T. Kirk's five-year mission, _U.S.S. Enterprise,_ NCC-1701.

2292

Alliance between the Klingon Empire and the Romulan Star Empire collapses.

2293

Colonel Worf, grandfather of Worf Rozhenko, defends Captain Kirk and Doctor McCoy at their trial for the murder of Klingon chancellor Gorkon.

Khitomer Peace Conference, Klingon Empire/Federation (_Star Trek VI_).

2323

Jean-Luc Picard enters Starfleet Academy's standard four-year program.

2328

The Cardassian Empire annexes the Bajoran homeworld.

2341

Data enters Starfleet Academy.

2342

Beverly Crusher (née Howard) enters Starfleet Academy Medical School, an eight-year program.

2346

Romulan massacre of Klingon outpost on Khitomer.

2351

In orbit around Bajor, the Cardassians construct a space station that they will later abandon.

2353

William T. Riker and Geordi La Forge enter Starfleet Academy.

2354

Deanna Troi enters Starfleet Academy.

2356

Tasha Yar enters Starfleet Academy.

2357

Worf Rozhenko enters Starfleet Academy.

2363

Captain Jean-Luc Picard assumes command of U.S.S. Enterprise, NCC-1701-D.

2367

Wesley Crusher enters Starfleet Academy.

An uneasy truce is signed between the Cardassians and the Federation.

Borg attack at Wolf 359; First Officer Lieutenant Commander Benjamin Sisko and his son, Jake, are among the survivors.

U.S.S. Enterprise-D defeats the Borg vessel in orbit around Earth.

2369

Commander Benjamin Sisko assumes command of Deep Space Nine in orbit over Bajor.

Source: Star Trek® Chronology / Michael Okuda and Denise Okuda

STARFALL

CHAPTER

1

Jean-Luc Picard was a failure.

He knew that at the very moment his computer screen blanked, with the TIME UP heading flashing at him in angry red. Around him, hopeful students sighed, groaned, or muttered. He did not dare look up. He felt his cheeks burn hot with shame.

Around him in the large San Francisco testing center, candidates had begun to converse nervously about their chances. He did not want to hear them. He switched off the power to his computer, got up, and went into the hall. He was high up, on the top floor of the fifteen-story Starfleet Records and Testing building. The window looked out across the bay to a gleaming complex of white buildings shining in the morning sun.

Starfleet Academy.

Jean-Luc balled his fists in frustration. This was as close as he would ever get—

Someone stuck his head out the door of the testing room and called, "Hey, you! Results are coming up."

Jean-Luc closed his eyes and took a deep breath. If only his mind had not been so preoccupied with what his father would say. If only he had gotten a decent night's sleep instead of staying awake trying desperately to cram a little more mathematics into his weary brain. If only—

"Are you coming?"

He grunted and turned. The big screen in the front of the testing room had come alive, showing the candidates' identification numbers and scores. A red line near the top of the list separated those who had passed the test and who qualified to go on to the next from the ones who had failed.

The ones like Jean-Luc.

His number glowed from just below the red line. So close, and yet he had not made it. He felt like hitting someone, preferably himself.

But the lucky ones who had passed were cheering and shaking hands. He forced a smile on his face, a smile that felt ghastly and masklike, and he extended his hand to congratulate a delirious young woman who had come in third.

Inside, though, he was thinking already of the humiliating trip back to France, back to the vineyard, back to the open scorn of a father who despised modern machinery. A father who, from the bottom of his soul, loathed Starfleet and all it stood for.

Jean-Luc did not know what he would say, what he would do, when he returned home tomorrow. He felt a rush of excuses—he was tired, he was worried, he was—

No. Face it. He was, purely and simply, a failure.

Long before Jean-Luc could see the vineyard, he could smell the young grapes. The fruity aroma was familiar to him, for he had spent all seventeen years of his life on his father's vineyard outside the village of LaBarre in France. Once he had liked the sweet, sharp scent, but on this hot summer day it almost made him sick.

His thoughts remained back in San Francisco, where he had spent three grinding days of testing. His stomach still felt twisted and painful, and the bitter taste of failure was still strong in his mouth.

The young man walked slowly, his thick brown hair lank with sweat. In his mind he relived the testing period that had made all the difference. Starfleet admissions standards were high, and of course the tests were difficult. And yet—

"I shouldn't have failed," Jean-Luc told himself in a voice of quiet fury. "I could do better. I *can* do better."

His heart beat faster with the humiliating memory. He scored second on most of the tests, third on a few others, before the humiliation of the advanced mathematics test and his horrible showing. Just afterward, before the candidates received appointments for the big stress test— the psychological exam that everyone dreaded—a kindly officer took him aside to tell him that his scores were

3

just a shade too low. "Don't feel bad," the officer had said with an encouraging smile. "You're only seventeen. Wait a year and try again. You'll be surprised at how much more you'll know then."

Jean-Luc clenched his teeth as he remembered the man's bland attempt to comfort him. *Wait a year!* Impossible. True, the man had no way of knowing that Jean-Luc had barely won permission from his father to try just this once, but still—

Something bounced off Jean-Luc's head, something thrown accurately but not so hard that it hurt. He spun around, raising his fists in anger.

"So you're not one of the walking dead after all," came the teasing voice of his older brother, Robert. He was sitting cross-legged atop a stone wall. He hopped down and strode toward Jean-Luc. "Oh, you're not going to hit me. Remember, Jean-Luc, you weren't the only one to win a medal for wrestling." Playfully Robert lunged at him.

Jean-Luc bounced back a step, dropped into a defensive crouch. He set his face in a stern mask of challenge. "Come and try me, Robert," he growled, his voice almost a snarl.

Robert raised his hands and grinned. "No, thank you very much." He rolled his eyes heavenward and heaved a deep sigh. "This is the thanks I get for being a considerate brother. I knew you'd be plodding back home, weary with disappointment, and I came to cheer you up—"

"By throwing rocks at me?" demanded Jean-Luc.

With a smirk Robert held up something that looked

4

like a little gray ball. It was a small mushroom. "Here's your rock," he said. "I picked these out of the moss behind the wall as you came trudging along with your head down and your gaze in the dirt. Did the great hard mushroom raise a lump, little brother?"

Jean-Luc snorted and strode away. He heard Robert's hurrying footsteps behind him, and a moment later he felt his brother's hand on his shoulder. "I'm sorry," Robert said, and he sounded sincere. "When you called, I could tell how disappointed you were. For what it's worth, Jean-Luc, I wish you *were* going to Starfleet Academy."

"It isn't fair," Jean-Luc said, his voice gruff. He was fighting the impulse to cry. "I could do better. I know I could. If only—"

The hand on his shoulder gave him an encouraging pat. "If only our father weren't so old-fashioned. If only you hadn't been worrying about how he would react to your passing the tests and leaving the vineyard. I know, Jean-Luc, I know."

After a few seconds of silence Jean-Luc said, "It isn't that I don't love Father."

"I know that, too, little brother. But you will admit, he can make himself a hard man to love. Ah, *voilà!* The new section."

The Picard vineyard covered many hectares, a countryside of rolling hillsides and thickly planted grape fields separated by rows of ancient oaks. The new section had been prepared for planting only the previous fall. Jean-Luc remembered the hours of back-straining labor to break the soil, to fertilize it, to prepare the land for the precious vines. All so senseless, when machines could do in a few hours the work he, his father, his brother, and their helpers did in weeks of groaning hard labor.

But such shortcuts were not for Maurice Picard, their proud and domineering father. Jean-Luc often thought that Maurice would have been happier in ancient times, as a vintner in fifteenth-century France, perhaps. Maurice always insisted that the old ways were the best ways, and he made sure that every step of growing grapes was done the old way.

Jean-Luc saw him now, a distant figure, measuring the tilled hillside for the arbors he and the boys would build that fall. The vines would begin to grow next year, and in a few year's time the new variety of Picard Rouge grape would yield its sweet juice. If everything had gone exactly right, if all the hard, hard work paid off, the juice would become a world-famous wine, just like Picard Noir. If not—well, one could always rip out the vines, rework the field, and replace the grapes with yet another variety.

"So much left to chance," murmured Jean-Luc. He halted, gazing off at the hillside and at his distant father.

"Chance?" asked Robert.

Jean-Luc shrugged and turned to walk toward the chateau. "Father hybridizes the grapes the old way. It would be so much easier to have a botanist genetically engineer a grape for whatever traits he wants. As it is, most of father's experiments are failures."

"Ah, yes, the Picards and their failures."

Jean-Luc froze in his tracks. "What did you say?"

"I said to get over your moping," Robert snapped.

"You promised Father that if you failed to get into Starfleet Academy, you'd drop the subject. Live up to your promise."

Jean-Luc did not answer. He stalked into the house, went straight to his room, and threw himself on his bed. His breath came painfully, and his throat ached from the effort not to sob. At last he sat up and looked around his familiar room. The ships in bottles, models that he had spent hours building, seemed meaningless and childish to him. Even the carefully modeled Promellian battle cruiser, the pride of his collection, looked like a stupid toy. What good were models when he wanted the real thing?

But his father would never consent to what Jean-Luc ached to ask him. "There's always next year," the officer had told him. And it was true enough that with a little more study, a little more application, his scores could improve. He was almost sure that he could pass the tests if he tried again next year. But he had promised his father. . . .

Jean-Luc remembered all too well how he had lost sleep before the first round of testing. He remembered, too, how satisfied Maurice had been when he had called home to confess his failure. "Good," his father had said with an air of finality. "I'm glad you have this Starfleet foolishness behind you. Now, if you want to attend a good agricultural college, I'd be happy to consider that— though they'd fill your head with all sorts of nonsense about bioengineering and technology. Well, spend a year or two on the vineyard, and then you'll know what you want to do."

8

Wrong, Father, thought Jean-Luc. *I don't need a year or two. I know what I want to do now. I always knew.*
I want to go to Starfleet Academy.
If only you would understand.

Jean-Luc felt no better that evening, when his mother called him and Robert to dinner. Yvette Picard's voice was musical and soft, and her manner was always elegant. Jean-Luc always thought that a woman like his mother should never have to worry about preparing meals, about cleaning a house; she should have replicators and machines to do all that. But Yvette loved Maurice and wanted to please him, and so every evening she prepared a meal the old-fashioned way.

And Jean-Luc had to admit that it was always delicious.

He slipped into his place at the table, the place beside his brother, where he had sat ever since outgrowing his high chair. Robert was there already, as tall as Jean-Luc and a little heavier, a little more muscular. The two boys had the same dark brown hair and the same determined cast of chin, inheritances from their mother and father. Maurice came in looking weary but happy. He settled into his place, the candlelight gleaming on his balding head. He murmured a brief grace, and then Yvette brought the meal in from the kitchen.

It was hearty fare: onion soup, thick with cheese, a green salad, coq au vin, the chicken replicated but the wine natural, and a delicate almond pastry for dessert. For a few moments they ate silently, and then Maurice looked up. "Well, now that both of our boys are here again, I have a surprise for the family," he said, a mischievous smile playing on his lips. "Some wonderful news."

They looked at him expectantly, but Maurice was in no hurry to reveal his surprise. "Jean-Luc," he said, "I know that sometimes you don't hear me say this enough, but I am very proud of you. Captain of your debate team, champion fencer, star marathon runner, valedictorian of your class . . . Son, I know how hard you have tried to please me. I'd like to please you as well, and I have been thinking over the question of how to do it very carefully. At last something occurred to me." He took a sip of wine, the Picard Noir 2315 that was in contention for this year's Grand Prix du Soleil, an award given to the wine named the very best in the entire Solar System. "I hope it will show you how much your efforts mean to me."

Jean-Luc's heart leaped. Did his father know that he wanted to test again for Starfleet Academy? Was he saying that he would give his consent? His mouth was dry with anticipation.

Maurice set down his wineglass. "I have agreed to buy the open lands to the east of the vineyards," he said. "I've gone over them carefully, and the soil is right for a white grape. We've never had a Picard Blanc, but I'm convinced we could produce an excellent one. We will increase the vineyard's size by nearly a third—and Jean-Luc, you will be in charge of all the new fields."

Jean-Luc choked. Beside him, Robert pushed his chair back and stood. "Father," his older brother said, anger hot in his voice, "you never told me about this."

Maurice's smile faded. "The opportunity arose suddenly," he said, his voice cold.

"But we were to be partners!" Robert said, his voice shrill with emotion. "I've worked this vineyard since I was ten—"

"And you've done a good job," Maurice said, a warning frown crossing his face. "But you won't begrudge a little glory to your younger brother—"

"Ha!" Robert scowled at Jean-Luc. "Begrudge a little glory! Father, when did he ever have anything but glory? He's the one you boast of, the one you pamper and spoil, and—"

"I won't have this talk," said Maurice, rising to his feet.

Yvette was standing, too. "Now, stop, the two of you," she said.

Jean-Luc could stand it no longer. He shouted, "Quiet, everyone!" They fell silent, looking at him in astonishment. "Doesn't it occur to anyone that *I* might have a word to say about all this?"

"The little mouse roars," said Robert bitterly. "Yes, tell us, Jean-Luc, in your wisdom, what is the perfect solution to this family disagreement?"

Jean-Luc felt his face burning. He hated these scenes. "First," he said, "I didn't ask Father for any new lands. I'm not sure I want to be in charge of anything like that—at least, not doing things your way, Father."

Maurice looked puzzled. "My way?"

"The old-fashioned way," Jean-Luc said, his voice tired. "I'm sorry, Father, but I don't want to—well, I—"

He took a deep breath. "I don't want to be a farmer at all! I want to go to Starfleet Academy and—"

"That's ridiculous!" Maurice bellowed angrily. "You ungrateful young fool!"

"I'm not," Jean-Luc protested. "I just want another chance to—"

"You'll get no other chances! Don't you know when you've failed? You weren't cut out to go gallivanting around in the stars. You have the vineyard, you have farming in your blood—what more do you want?"

"I want what's right for me!"

"I'll tell you what's right for you!"

The furious argument that followed sent Jean-Luc stalking to his room, back rigid, jaw clenched. He hurled himself onto his bed, his eyes burning, his throat pain-

12

fully clenched against rising sobs. He told himself with fierce pride that he would not let himself cry.

He fell asleep on the bed, fully clothed, and woke sometime late at night, aware that someone else was in the room. He began to sit up, but a cool hand pressed against his forehead.

"Quiet, quiet," his mother said. "I didn't mean to wake you."

Jean-Luc lay back. His face seemed tight, and he could feel that tears had dried on his cheeks. "Oh, Mother," he said miserably, "how will I ever live?"

"You will find your own way," Yvette replied at once. "Jean-Luc, tonight you surprised me."

"I know," he groaned. "I honestly tried not to mention Starfleet, but—"

"Oh, Starfleet," she said, dismissing the idea. "No, you surprised me by how much you are like Robert and your father. Proud, strong, independent—or, to put it another way, pigheaded and stubborn. You've always been the quiet one, but I knew the Picard in you would come to the surface eventually." She leaned close and kissed him on the forehead. "You get some sleep. I shouldn't have come in."

"What will I do?" Jean-luc asked as she rose from his bedside.

Her voice came from the dark, firm and full of love: "Why, Jean-Luc, you will do what you must do. That, too, is the Picard in you." The door opened and closed softly.

Jean-Luc rose in the dark, changed his clothes, and opened the window. He stared out into a night full of brilliant starlight. He looked up at the stars for a long time, feeling a hopeless yearning. They were so far away. Between him and the stars lay the barriers of failure and a promise that he hated but must keep. The stars offered no help, just their cold, eternal, mocking light. At last, exhausted, he fell back into bed and into a deep sleep, dreaming himself onto the bridge of a starship.

CHAPTER

2

The next day Jean-Luc used their home terminal, one of the few modern conveniences that Maurice grudgingly allowed the household. He requested a copy of the mathematics examination, printed it, and took it to his room. Odd how easy some of the questions appeared now. Frowning, Jean-Luc went through them the old-fashioned way, with a pencil and paper. He saw small errors that he had made, errors of carelessness and of exhaustion. If he had the test to take over again, he knew that he could pass it.

Over the next few weeks he began to study, late at night, after the work on the farm had been done. Now that he had seen what the testing was like, he realized minor ways he had gone wrong. Without speaking to anyone about his project, Jean-Luc began to train himself, not the frantic last-minute cramming that had done him in, but a long, steady haul. It was like training for a race, done a little at a time. Although he had no plans to retest for Starfleet, somehow studying helped to ease his pain at failing. And distracted him from the fact that half a planet away, Starfleet Academy was beginning a new year . . . without him.

Not that he neglected working on the vineyard. If anything, he plunged into that with even fiercer determination. Somehow, whenever he concentrated only on the farm chores that had to be done, he even pleased his father, for Jean-Luc was a hard worker, and he succeeded at everything he tried.

Almost everything.

At the bottom of his memory, like a bitter, rotten grape, was the sour memory of his biggest failure—practically his only failure. When he was working or studying, he rarely thought of it. When he was idle, the memory burned in him. So he tried running away from it. In high school Jean-Luc had been a track star and a marathon runner. For a month or two after graduation he fell out of training, but one morning in September, almost out of his mind with boredom, he put on his running shoes. That day he did a hard five kilometers, running all out until he was ready to fall over from weariness. Even so, that night, like every night, he hit the books again, learning about Cochrane physics and temporal distortion, about inertia fields and astronavigation. As he was falling asleep, the thought came to him that the preparation had to be for something.

16

He knew then that he was going to reapply to the Academy.

He suspected the rage that Maurice would show when he learned of his son's decision. Should he tell his father? No, he decided on the very edge of sleep. Right now they were all happy, or reasonably happy. There was no reason to spoil that by telling about his plans.

Not yet, anyway. Not just yet.

Beginning the next morning he ran every day, all through winter, and now into a bright but cool May. Before reporting to the fields, he left the vineyard at dawn, ran all the way to LaBarre and now was almost back, pacing himself for the last long hill. Physically he felt wonderful—if only his problems had been physical, he thought, he would have nothing to regret, nothing to complain about.

He saw Robert sitting on the stone wall ahead and to his right, and he had a quick flash of déjà vu, that creepy feeling that he was reliving a moment. Then he remembered that this was the very place where Robert had greeted him last summer on his return from his testing.

Robert hopped lightly off the wall and dropped into step beside Jean-Luc, loping along easily, although he was long out of practice as a runner. "I got my answer from Father at last," Robert told Jean-Luc, pleasure in his voice. "He said yes at breakfast this morning."

"Oh?" gasped Jean-Luc. "Then you're going off-world?"

"To Alkalurops Beta Two," Robert confirmed. "At the end of the summer. I'll spend a whole year there learning about their growing techniques."

17

"Lucky for you they don't use machinery." Jean-Luc was really too winded to talk, but he didn't want to show any weakness to his older brother. They came in sight of the chateau, and Jean-Luc slowed to a walk. He needed to cool down and to do his stretching exercises.

Robert hadn't run far enough to trouble with that, but he walked alongside anyway. "Lucky for me you are so indispensable," he muttered, his voice now irritable. "Father doesn't need me at all with you around."

"That isn't true," Jean-Luc snapped. "You can do everything I do. You even like it."

"Tell *him* that," Robert said moodily.

"I have." Jean-Luc almost added, "Soon he'll have to do without both of us," but he had not yet applied for retesting, and he knew that speaking of it to Robert would be the same as telling Maurice. He kept quiet. For a few minutes they walked silently, and then Jean-Luc halted to stretch his leg muscles. He felt the old familiar glow that running always gave him, the feeling of health and ease. Robert leaned against a fence, arms crossed, staring at him.

"Well," Jean-Luc said, "at last you get to do something you've wanted."

Robert nodded but did not smile. "That's true. You know, when I graduated from high school, Father promised that I could go to college anywhere I wanted. But first, he said, I had to work on the vineyard because you were still in school and he couldn't be short-handed. Well, I waited for three years, and then you graduated. And now it's taken me most of another year to talk him into keeping his promise."

18

"Alkalurops Beta Two is a planet, not a college," Jean-Luc pointed out. He was doing toe touches, and his hair kept flopping into his eyes. He had grown careless about keeping it trimmed.

"I know that," returned Robert. "But it's an educational planet."

Jean-Luc merely grunted. He knew that Alkalurops Beta II was a sparsely populated colony world, home to a human population of only five million. A very few Vulcans lived there, too, in one small community, and a sprinkling of other aliens owned businesses in the larger towns. But the planet was almost entirely an agricultural paradise, growing quintotriticale, other grains, and a bewildering variety of fruits and vegetables, some native to the planet, others imported from Earth and elsewhere. The land masses of the planet, its distance from its sun— everything came together to make the world ideal for those who loved the land and the things it produced. Robert was right. He would learn lots of things from his year on Alkalurops Beta II.

"I want you to know something," Robert said as Jean-Luc finished his exercises. "This is something I've had my heart set on for a long time."

Jean-Luc stared at his brother. The morning light was full in Robert's face, and with a shock, Jean-Luc noticed that Robert's hair was thinning. His scalp glowed through the sparse hair at the crown of his head. The light and shadows on Robert's face made him look far older than twenty, made him look a lot like Maurice. "I know you've been waiting for the chance," Jean-Luc said. "I wish you well. Truly."

"Thank you, little brother," Robert said. He smiled, and the illusion of age dropped away. He was himself again, the big brother who had taught Jean-Luc how to swim, who had cheered him on in fencing matches and debate contests. "I know you won't do anything to spoil my chance."

Jean-Luc felt puzzled. "What? Of course I won't, but what makes you think that I *could* spoil your chance? Father promised you that you could go."

Robert gave him an ironic smile. "Yes, he did. He would change his mind, though, if you should talk of leaving. I'd never get away then."

Jean-Luc felt an icy shiver of premonition. "What are you asking me to do, Robert?"

Robert looked away. "To forget about Starfleet Academy," he said in a low voice. "For this year, anyway."

Jean-Luc bit his lip. He had said nothing about the Academy for months, and he certainly had kept his studies a complete secret. "Does it still show?" he asked.

"What? That you want to be in Starfleet? You can't disguise that, Jean-Luc. Only wait a year—that's all I'm asking. Wait just one more year before you ask Father's permission to test again."

A whole year! The nine months since last summer seemed almost endless to Jean-Luc. How could he promise to wait for another year? He shook his head. "I'm sorry, Robert. I know how much this means to you, but—"

Robert's face flushed red with anger. "Sometimes I hate you," he snarled, and he turned and strode off.

Jean-Luc sighed. He loved his brother, but there were

times when the two couldn't stand each other. Yet there were so many good times, so many long days in the vineyard, so many refreshing swims in the river, so much joking and laughter—it was all too confusing. He didn't know if—

"Jean-Luc!" The familiar voice broke into his thoughts, made him look up sharply.

Louis, of course, laughing, husky Louis Blanchard, hopping out of his sleek silver aircar. He had landed expertly, so quietly that Jean-Luc hadn't even noticed his approach. Louis came bouncing over to him, energy in every step, a beaming smile on his face. "What, running again?"

"You should try it," Jean-Luc said, grinning at the overflowing good spirits of his best friend. "You're going to get fat riding around in that machine all the time."

Louis slapped his flat stomach. "Me? Impossible! I'm in better shape than ever." Louis had also been a runner in high school, though his specialty was sprints rather than distance running. That was typical of him—he had boundless energy for short bursts, but he found it hard to stick with something like a long project or a marathon run. "Hey, I've come to offer you the opportunity of a lifetime."

"Right now the only opportunity I want is to shower and change clothes," Jean-Luc returned. "Come on in, though. Have you had breakfast? Of course you have. You're always up with the dawn. Well, you can have a cup of chocolate while I eat, and then you can tell me about this wonderful opportunity."

Jean-Luc hurried through his shower. His father was

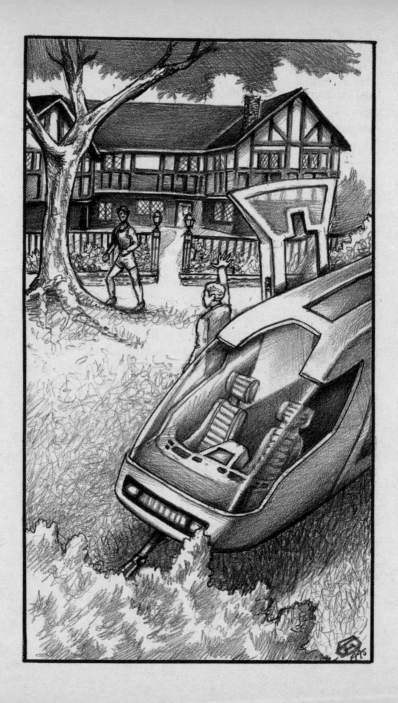

already out in the vineyard, and he supposed that Robert was there, too. He wouldn't be expected or needed for a while—the vines required little attention at this time of year. It would be later, with the autumn harvest, that the work would stretch into twelve and fourteen hour days. He prepared himself a light breakfast, a croissant and hot, dark chocolate, and sat with Louis at the table. "Now," he said, "what's your news? Have you finally decided what your college major will be?"

Louis grinned. He was a dark-haired young man the same age as Jean-Luc, slightly shorter, slightly more heavily built. "Now, now," he said. "It isn't unusual for a student to spend his first year in general studies. I'm still casting about for my life's work," Louis had a wonderful mind, and he could have gone to any university on or off Earth, but he settled for a year at the local campus of the European University. Unlike Jean-Luc, Louis had no clear idea of what he wanted to be or study. He sipped his chocolate and said, "I'm beginning to think that hydroponics is my field."

Jean-Luc laughed. "And last week it was xenobiology, and the month before it was linguistics."

"No, this time I'm serious," Louis insisted.

Jean-Luc shook his head. "Really, Louis, growing food without soil is incredibly important to colony worlds and to deep space stations, but isn't it rather, well, boring?"

"Ha," Louis retorted. "You and your dirt-grubbing farmboy ways! Why, there are all sorts of challenges and opportunities in the field. Did you know that . . ."

For the next ten minutes Louis lectured him on botany, growth coefficients, and ecology. At last Jean-Luc raised his hands in mock surrender. "Enough!" he pleaded. "Louis, that's all very well for you, but what about the opportunity you were going to give *me?* I haven't heard anything about that yet!"

"Oh," Louis said. "Right. Sorry. Well, do you know what Medlab-One is?"

Jean-Luc rolled his eyes. "Would it happen to be an experimental undersea colony on the floor of the Mediterranean?" he asked sarcastically. "The place where scientists are studying ways to establish human colonies on worlds that are all ocean? Or is there some other Medlab-One I haven't heard about?"

"All right, all right," said Louis. "So you know about Medlab. I'll bet you didn't know this, though: It includes a self-contained university, with degree-granting privileges and everything. Every summer Medlab has orientation sessions for prospective students who want to learn more about their techniques and methods. And I've asked them to save two spots, beginning two weeks from Monday. One for you and one for me. What do you say to a week's Mediterranean vacation?"

Jean-Luc couldn't help himself. He burst into laughter. Louis looked hurt. "S-sorry, Louis," Jean-Luc gasped at last. "I was just thinking of your, ah, skill at swimming, and—and it seemed so funny that—" he dissolved into laughter again.

Louis sniffed. "Some people don't take to the water," he observed.

Jean-Luc wiped his eyes with his napkin. "No," he said, "they certainly don't. What did Coach Deitz compare your crawl stroke to? 'A hippopotamus with a stomachache,' wasn't it? Louis, you can hardly swim!"

"They have aquatracs," Louis said. "You don't need to swim. You just need to be able to use an air tank and to hang on to your aquatrac."

"I'm sorry," Jean-Luc said with a grin. "Look, how long did you say this trip will last?"

"One week," Louis returned, his high spirits flooding back. He almost bounced in his chair. "We'd get a complete tour of all the facilities, and lots of time off. And, Jean-Luc, about half the students touring are always girls!"

"And you look so handsome in swimming trunks," Jean-Luc said.

"Well, I'd argue with you, but that happens to be true," responded Louis. "Come on, Jean-Luc. Wouldn't you like to get away from here for a week?"

For more than that, thought Jean-Luc with a little stab of conscience. But then he considered the possibility. Perhaps this trip could be the excuse he had been searching for. One didn't just transmit an application to test for Starfleet Academy; that had to be done in person. And while promising high-school students always made the trip to San Francisco, there was also a smaller European testing center near Paris. That would be much more discreet. If Louis had timed things a little better, Jean-Luc might even have gotten away with the actual testing with no one's being the wiser. However—

"We'll need to talk more about this later. But I'll ask," he said at last. He went in search of his mother and found her at the household computer terminal, shopping.

Most houses had more than one computer, more than one holophone. The old-fashioned Maurice permitted just one of each, both of them in the little office off the kitchen. Yvette looked up and smiled as he came in.

"Good morning," she said. "Jean-Luc, have we had quiche too often to consider it again? I can't decide how much cheese to order."

"Your quiche is always delicious," Jean-Luc said with a smile. "There's never any left, is there?"

"Well, that's true." She ordered the cheese and said, "What's on your mind, Jean-Luc?"

Jean-Luc told her about Louis and his offer. She nodded and gave him an understanding look. "I think that's a splendid idea. You've worked hard, and you deserve some time off. Go ahead, Jean-Luc."

"I haven't asked Father," he said with some reluctance.

She reached out and touched his hand lightly. "He won't mind," she assured him. "Tell Louis of course you'll go. And while you're away, try to enjoy yourself."

Jean-Luc kissed his mother on the cheek and went to tell Louis that he would go. Louis slapped him on the back and then hurried out to his aircar. Jean-Luc saw him off, then stood there until the car was a gleaming silver dot racing off toward LaBarre. He hoped that the deceptions he was planning would work out all right. Louis would not be angry with him. Perhaps, if he succeeded, neither would his father.

With a bitter grin Jean-Luc shook his head.

No. Nothing could save him from his father's anger.

CHAPTER

3

Louis stared at his friend. "You're not going?" he yelped, his voice rising with disbelief.

The other young people in the waiting area looked around at them. Jean-Luc spoke in a whisper: "I'm not. I'll see you off, though, and then I'm going to Paris. I have business there."

Louis gave him a hard, suspicious look. The two of them sat at an umbrella-shaded table on a wharf at Marseilles. The Mediterranean sparkled beyond, green close in to shore, a brilliant blue farther out. A hundred young men and women were gathered on benches, at other tables, waiting for the hovercraft that would take them out to Medlab-1. Jean-Luc had waited until they were well away from LaBarre before telling Louis his plan. Now he waited for his friend's reaction. After a long moment Louis said, "You're going to do it, aren't you? You're going to apply for retesting to Starfleet Academy."

Jean-Luc nodded.

Louis sighed. "You have a lot of courage, Jean-Luc."

"No more than you." Jean-Luc gestured at the sea. "You're going down to live forty meters below the surface, and you swim only a little better than a rock."

"There are dangers and then there are dangers," Louis returned in a moody growl.

"Jean-Luc? I thought that was you. Remember me?"

A pretty blond girl had walked over to their table and now stood with her hands on her hips and a broad smile on her freckled face.

Jean-Luc recognized her at once. With an answering smile, he cleared his throat and in his best debate-team manner said, "Resolved: Kimberly Bloom is the most attractive student to take this tour. I take the affirmative."

She took the chair next to Louis, laughing and holding out her hand for Jean-Luc to shake. She was radiantly beautiful, blue-eyed, with a lively face made interesting by those few freckles splashed across the bridge of her nose. "Took you long enough to spot me, mate," she said, her Australian accent as strong as he remembered it. "I thought you'd blinking well forgotten me."

"Oh, I never forget anyone who scores more points than I do," Jean-Luc said with a rueful grin. "Kimberly, this is my friend Louis Blanchard. Louis, Kimberly Bloom, who led the All-Australia Debate Team last year at the Hemisphere finals."

"And who squeaked out a win over the Western European Team," Kimberly said. "Hi, Louis. So you're along for the undersea trip, too. Isn't this great?"

"It sure is," Louis said, staring at her.

"I'm just here to see Louis off," Jean-Luc quickly explained.

Kimberly smiled at Louis.

"Hey, tell you what—I'll get my gear and we'll hang out together. I was afraid I'd be all alone this trip. It's wonderful to have friends about." She sprang up and walked away.

Beyond her, Jean-Luc saw a white craft coming in fast toward the wharf. He got to his feet. "Well, this is where I leave you. Louis?"

"Hmm?" Louis murmured. He was still staring at Kimberly, who was busily gathering up her luggage.

"You be careful," Jean-Luc said, grinning at his friend. "I've never seen you this dumbstruck before."

"Jean-Luc," moaned Louis, "that's because I've never been in love before!"

Paris in May was a beautiful old city, but Jean-Luc hardly noticed it. He spent three days in the Paris Xenology Library, the most complete collection of information on alien life and planets that Earth possessed. He methodically arranged to have book after book transmitted to his home over the computer network, knowing that each one would help his chances of passing the exams. Of course, he carefully arranged to have transmission begin only after he planned to be back in LaBarre. It wouldn't do for Maurice to demand why he was doing all this reading on Vulcan philosophy, Klingon military organization, and Andorian technology.

Finally, on the fourth day of his stay, Jean-Luc worked up the nerve to take a short walk from his hotel, really just around the block. He had chosen his hotel for this one purpose, after all. Now he plucked up all of his courage to follow through with his plan.

The local applications office for Starfleet Academy was hardly more than a small room divided in half by a chest-high counter. One woman worked there, a grandmotherly type who wore the silver-and-gray uniform of a retired Starfleet engineering officer. "May I help you?" she asked with a smile as Jean-Luc came in from the sunny street.

"Ah—are there any openings left for the July testing period?" Jean-Luc heard himself ask.

"I'm sorry," she said, making his heart sink. "If you want to test at the main center, you have to apply four months in advance."

"No," Jean-Luc said hurriedly. "No, I don't have to go to San Francisco. I thought maybe the local center was—might have a space or two—"

She looked at him. "You realize that all the secondary testing areas have a pretty strict quota system. Really, one must score more highly at the European center than at the main location to be considered for admission."

"Yes, I know that," Jean-Luc said. He had studied the statistics carefully. The secondary centers, in Europe, Asia, Australia, and South America, were always the choice of the tentative candidates. Not many of them ever made it into the Academy. Those who were more sure of themselves always went to San Francisco for the tests. Jean-Luc said, "I do mean to pass. I couldn't apply earlier for the main center because of—of family problems." It was true, in a way. Maurice *was* family, and he *was* a problem.

"I see. Well, let me check the records." The woman tapped a computer board and glanced at a display screen. "You're in luck," she said, her tone surprised and at least a little pleased. "We have one position open. Do you want an application form?"

Jean-Luc had not expected his throat to be so dry. He licked his lips. "Yes, please."

She handed him a computer padd. "You can sit over there to fill out the form," she said, pointing to a small booth in the corner. "Good luck."

Good luck, indeed, thought Jean-Luc. If his father ever found out about this, he would need all the good luck in the world and then some.

He began to enter his name on the application form and tried to get over the feeling as he added each letter that he was making the biggest mistake of his life.

"You were in *Madrid?*" asked Louis, looking baffled. "I thought you were going to Paris!"

"I did, for four days," Jean-Luc patiently explained. "Then I spent the next two at the Madrid Technological Center, studying the application of Cochrane fields and warp drives. And how was your stay in Medlab?"

Louis could not keep a grin from his face. "Marvelous! I've been accepted for the autumn term. Kimberly may apply later. They accept students right up to August, and she hasn't made up her mind yet. Oh, she wants me to ask you something."

Jean-Luc had met Louis at the Marseilles dock. Now the two of them were waiting for the shuttle that would take them on the short flight back to LaBarre. The terminal was a busy one, with travelers bustling to and fro, and the two of them had settled on a bench in an out-of-the-way corner to get their stories set.

"What does Kimberly want?" Jean-Luc asked.

"Well, she has a twin sister."

"I know. She spoke about her when we talked at the debate tournament. What's her name?"

"Melissa. Misty for short."

Jean-Luc nodded, remembering the name now. "Interested in computer science, isn't she?"

"Yes, studying at Melbourne. Anyway, she's coming to Paris next month, and the two of them are going to take a cycling tour of France. They want us to come along."

With a tilt of his head Jean-Luc glanced at his friend. "I don't think I can," he said.

Louis made a face. "Oh, come on. Kim talked of you the whole time. It would be a lot of fun, and, uh, I really want to go. I mean, I *really,* really want to go."

Laughing, Jean-Luc said, "Maybe you'd better not. I'd say you were pretty far gone already."

"What?"

"Look, I have lots of preparation to do in the next month, all sorts of things to learn. I'm sorry, Louis, but I can't make the trip."

"Then I'll have to go with them on my own," Louis said. "What a tragedy!"

"That's your choice," said Jean-Luc. "I'm warning you, though, be very careful. If Misty is anything like her sister, you're going to be head over heels with both of them."

"That is a cutting remark," Louis returned with dignity. "Just because I value Kim's friendship doesn't mean I feel romantic about her. And even if I did, I wouldn't feel the same way about her sister. And besides—"

"There's the shuttle," Jean-Luc said, standing. "Very well, do whatever you want. But on the way home, do me a big favor and tell me all about our trip to Medlab-One. When my parents ask me what we did there, I want to be able to give them some believable answers!"

"All right, all right," said Louis as they walked toward the boarding gate. "First of all, Kim Bloom looks absolutely stunning in a bathing suit. . . ."

On the flight home Jean-Luc learned lots more. Unfortunately, hardly any of it had to do with Medlab-1.

CHAPTER

4

June began with the usual summer chores to be done on a vineyard run on old-fashioned principles. Jean-Luc, Robert, and Maurice spent hour after hour in the sun inspecting the vines, making sure the clusters of swelling grapes were well-supported on their arbors, looking for telltale spots that would mark the onslaught of disease, fungus, or insect parasites. When they found anything suspicious, they had to go to work at once to cure the disease, stop the fungus, remove the parasites.

It would be so easy, Jean-Luc thought for the thousandth time, *to rig biofield generators to keep out pests and to neutralize fungus spores and bacteria.* But that would be an invasion of the sacred vineyard by technology, and Maurice wouldn't hear of it.

For his part, Maurice was exceptionally cheerful. The harvest promised to be a bountiful one, much larger than the vineyard had ever before produced. Even better, the Picard Noir 2316 had proved to be a superb vintage. It was even superior to the wonderful 2315. Last year Maurice had lost the Prix du Soleil to an Italian competitor who grew his grapes on the Cortez space station, with all the help that technology could give him. Maurice took some comfort in the fact that it was a hard decision; it took the judges an unusually long time to decide. This year, Maurice thought, the coveted award was his. He was already planning his trip to Paris for the official tasting and awards ceremony.

And so June went on, day after sweltering day, with both brothers and their father hard at work. If Jean-Luc seemed more exhausted than usual, why, that was only to be expected. His later hours could be chalked up to his youth. If he labored in his room to build a perfect model of the *Orlando,* a Constellation-class starship, that was only recreation. It certainly could not be called studying—even if the model was complete down to the Jeffries tubes and the antimatter containment field cores. If on the weekends Jean-Luc took the family aircar apart and then reassembled it, that was simply an excess of youthful energy. It couldn't have anything to do with practical and applied engineering skills.

Or at least that was what Jean-Luc hoped his father would think. Maurice seemed not to notice, even though once or twice Jean-Luc caught suspicious glances from his brother. Robert, who occasionally used the holophone and the computer terminals, could hardly fail to

see that Jean-Luc's computer files had swollen to hundreds of times their normal size. But if he suspected his brother was up to something, at least Robert had the grace not to mention it. And anyway, Robert, just like Jean-Luc, was overworked and tired.

Finally, toward the middle of the month, they all met in late afternoon after a long day in the vineyard, all of them sweating from the hot summer sun. Their labor had paid off, though, for the vineyard was in excellent shape, the vines heavy with their burdens of ripening grapes. Maurice clapped both his sons on the back. "Better and better," he boomed. "And next year we'll have the white grapes as well. Think what that means!"

"We'll need more help," Jean-Luc said.

"Oh, rubbish. We can handle the work. We're Picards!" Maurice said with his deep laugh. "Three strong backs, three sharp minds. Like the Three Musketeers, aren't we?"

"Father," Robert said gently, "I won't be here next year, remember?"

Maurice grinned at his son. "Well, maybe you won't be, and maybe you will. Who knows? If things turn out as well as I think, I may just have to call you back from Alkalurops Beta Two six months early. You wouldn't want to miss the summer and autumn, anyway. It will be a grand harvest!"

Robert's face set itself in a grim expression. "I won't be able to complete my course of study in only six months," he said. "There's no sense in going at all if I can't earn my diploma. Father, you'd better make other plans."

"You'll come round," Maurice insisted. "This is your home, where your roots are. You mark my words. When you get word of how the vineyard thrives this next year, how heavy the vines will be, you'll *want* to return for the harvest."

"Robert wouldn't have to come back early. We could bring in more help," Jean-Luc said in a tentative voice. "I'm sure lots of the high-school students would like to come after school to learn—"

"Amateurs!" Maurice bellowed, though still in a tone of high good humor. "Jean-Luc, you can't trust grapes to just anyone. They have to be pampered by people who love and understand them."

"There's always automation," Jean-Luc said.

His father gave him a playful rap on the shoulder. "Now you're just trying to make the old man angry, and I won't be angry on such a beautiful day. No, we Picards can take care of the vineyard all by ourselves, without any help from amateurs, either flesh-and-blood or electronic."

"You and Jean-Luc can take care of it, you mean," Robert insisted bitterly. "Don't count on having me back, Father. Of course, it's well known that little brother can do the work of any two men, so you don't need to worry about it. You won't need me at all."

Maurice stared at his elder son. "You'll think better of it," he said and turned abruptly. He strode away, leaving the two brothers at the edge of the southern field.

"Don't set him off," Jean-Luc warned Robert. "He'll forget about ordering you home early if you don't argue with him. But you know how he is when you oppose

38

him. What are you angry about, anyway? You're going to be going off-world soon."

"Oh, get out of my sight," Robert growled.

Jean-Luc felt anger hot inside him, like a tight ball of fire. With an effort he controlled his temper. *Maybe a run would help,* he thought. A nice *long* one. He went back to his room, changed from his working clothes to a T-shirt and running shorts, pulled out a well-broken-in pair of running shoes, and then rummaged in a dresser drawer for a sweatband and wristbands. He paused in the kitchen to fill a liter bottle with water. He was ready for a long run.

He spent some minutes stretching out, then set off at an easy pace. It was a hot summer afternoon, and soon his headband was soggy. He felt the air cooling the sweat on his face, arms, and legs. He began to tire, as he always did, and to feel an ache in his thighs. He ignored everything. Before long he gained his second wind. This was what he ran for: that wonderful moment when new strength came flooding into his weary legs, when it seemed he never had to stop but could just keep on running forever. He settled his stride into a comfortable, smooth, kilometer-eating pace and cleared his mind of everything but the pathway.

By the time Jean-Luc returned to the vineyard the back way, down the lane that divided the new land from the old, more than three hours had passed. The sun had already set, but a bright summer twilight lingered in the west. Jean-Luc estimated that he had run twenty kilometers or so, no marathon but a good solid workout anyway. He felt tired but happy. He slowed to a walk to cool down, and when he came to the chateau, he was breathing normally and all but glowing from his run.

Robert banged out of the house and came straight for him, his face dark with anger. Jean-Luc blinked at him, startled. "What—"

Robert pushed his shoulder hard, making him stagger back a step. "You ran away. You left me to deal with him. Why are you always the perfect one?" He shoved him again, so hard that Jean-Luc almost fell backward.

"Stop it," Jean-Luc snapped. "I don't even know what you're upset about."

"What do you think?" Robert charged him.

Jean-Luc, taken off guard, stumbled back and fell under his brother's weight. "Come on!" grunted Robert. "Fight!"

Very well. Robert was trying to pin him down, as if they were in a wrestling match. But Jean-Luc's arms were slick with sweat, and Robert couldn't keep his hold. Jean-Luc squirmed enough to bend his leg, and he used Robert's momentum to flip him over. Both of them scrambled up at once. Robert, heavier and more solid, lunged again. Jean-Luc, lighter and more agile, dodged him.

They circled, crouching. Robert feinted to the right, and Jean-Luc instinctively dodged, but Robert had planned the move well. He seized Jean-Luc in an expert half nelson and tried to force him to his knees.

Jean-Luc knew a way to break the hold, but it required both strength and quickness, and his run had left him tired. He pivoted, bent, and tried to throw Robert off him, but failed. Robert was grunting with effort now, pressing him toward the ground.

One last hope. Jean-Luc guessed where Robert's feet were planted, set his right foot, and attempted a backward sweep with his left leg. He connected, and Robert toppled, losing his hold. But he was up again in an instant, charging forward to tackle Jean-Luc at the waist. The impact sent them both rolling on the ground.

Then suddenly their mother was there, yelling, "Stop this!" at the top of her lungs. She was usually so quiet that the shout had the effect of a gunshot. Both Jean-Luc and Robert froze in position, and then they rolled apart and got to their feet.

Yvette Picard was standing with her hands on her hips. Her eyes flashed with anger. "You two should be ashamed."

Robert slapped some of the dirt from his trousers. "Good thing you stopped us," he growled. "No doubt the wrestling champion would have beaten me senseless." He turned and walked away, just as Maurice had walked away from the two brothers earlier that day.

Jean-Luc was panting for breath. Yvette scowled at him. "Are you all right?"

Jean-Luc nodded. "What's wrong with him?" he asked. "I just came in, and he jumped me."

"Walk with me," Yvette said. They went behind the chateau, toward the ancient foundations of stables and outbuildings that once had been attached to the house. Twilight was deepening. Venus shone clear and bright in the west, a dazzling white point of light, and a few stars were beginning to appear. Yvette and Jean-Luc came to

41

the old brick well, which Maurice had repaired. It was really only decorative, but it still worked. Yvette lowered the bucket by means of a sweep, a long lever arrangement right out of the Middle Ages. She brought the wooden bucket up dripping and said, "Here."

Jean-Luc drank the cold water gratefully, slopping some of it down his front. He had long before emptied his water bottle, and the well water was refreshing and welcome, tasting of iron and the earth. "Thank you," he said.

"Your father will win the Prix du Soleil this year. That means a great deal to him."

"I know."

Yvette went to a stone bench near the well. A trellis of roses grew beside it, and she sat beneath the flowers. After a moment she patted the bench. "Come and sit with me."

Jean-Luc sank onto the stone seat. His muscles ached from his run and from the fight. The sweet, strong odor of roses was almost overpowering. "What's wrong with Robert?" he asked.

"He had words with your father, of course," Yvette answered with a sigh. "Do you understand why he's so upset, Jean-Luc?"

"Because Father said he will bring him back from his trip early. But that's not my fault."

"That isn't the reason."

For a few minutes they sat in silence. The evening sky grew darker, and a meteorite traced a brilliant path across the heavens. "What's the reason?" Jean-Luc asked eventually, as if they had been talking all along.

42

"What do you think?"

"I don't know, Mother." Jean-Luc couldn't keep all the sarcasm out of his voice. "What does Robert want from me? Doesn't he know that I've given up my biggest dream to stay here on the vineyard with Father? Does he think I like this?"

"Your brother has his dreams, too," Yvette said quietly. "Can't you understand what they are, Jean-Luc?"

"To go to Alkalurops Beta Two and study viniculture. That's what he says."

"He says that because the truth hurts him."

After another long pause Jean-Luc said slowly, "I always thought that Robert was just like Father. That he wanted to stay on the vineyard and manage it. That he wanted to win prizes for his wines."

"I believe you're right."

"Well, what's stopping him?" Jean-Luc asked angrily.

"You."

The word hit Jean-Luc hard. He looked up at the sky. Another meteorite flashed, and another.

When he had been silent for a long time, Yvette said, "There are a lot of shooting stars tonight."

"Starfleet did that," Jean-Luc replied at once. "There was an asteroid in an orbit that threatened to crash it into Earth. Starfleet vaporized it last year. The meteorites are the tiny grains and particles that were left over from the explosion. We'll have several meteor showers this summer." Jean-Luc remembered something else. "When they announced it on the news, someone said the season's name should be changed this year from 'summer' to "starfall.' "

43

"Starfall. Not a bad name. Yes, now I remember hearing about that on the news."

Jean-Luc's mind was not on shooting stars. "Mother, what did you mean? I'm not stopping Robert. I wish he would take charge of the vineyard. I only want to—to be left out of it."

"But that isn't the way your father sees it," Yvette told him. "Maurice has his dreams, too. You must understand, Jean-Luc, he is very proud of you. You're the genius of the family. He believes you could do great things with the vineyard, wonderful things. That's why he's getting you ready to inherit it, to run it."

"I don't want to do that!"

"And Robert does," Yvette reminded him. "That's why he was fighting you. You have everything that Robert would like to have, and you don't even want it. Robert sees you and knows how happy he would be in your place. That makes him angry."

"It isn't my fault."

"No one said it was. Look! It's like fireworks."

Jean-Luc stared into the darkening sky. It was a riot of meteor trails, some dazzling tracks that lingered for seconds after the passage of the meteorites, some flickering traces of yellow or red. All he could think about was the Starfleet ship, just a small craft with a crew of five, that had destroyed the asteroid back in November. To the five crew members, that would have been a very routine mission, in Earth's own backyard. Just something to take up a day or two, and then on to other things.

To Jean-Luc, it would have been the adventure of a lifetime.

44

Yvette said, "Your father and I will go to Paris next week for the awards ceremony. I think you should come along."

"Why?"

His mother's voice was soft. "It is important for a family to be together at times. Especially when one—or more—of the family will be leaving soon. Will you come along on the trip?"

Jean-Luc took a deep breath. He wondered if his mother had guessed what he had done. She certainly knew that he had spent late hours with the computer, that he read far into the night. He felt an urge to confess everything to her, to tell her that he had already applied to retest for the Academy. He wondered if he dared.

The sky went wild with a fall of stars.

CHAPTER

5

In the glare of a spotlight the master of ceremonies opened an envelope. "This year's Grand Prix du Soleil is awarded by unanimous decision," he read, "to..." The audience stirred as the man prolonged the wait. "To Maurice Picard for Picard Noir, vintage 2316."

A thousand pairs of hands applauded. Maurice, his face red with pleasure, pushed back his chair and made a stiff bow, then moved to the lectern. Yvette, Robert, and Jean-Luc applauded him, though Jean-Luc was thinking how unusual his father looked in formal wear instead of farming clothes.

"Thank you," Maurice murmured as the master of ceremonies slipped the red, white, and blue ribbon over his head. The gold medallion, a smiling sunface, blazed on his chest.

Maurice blinked into the light, smiling and nodding. When the applause had faded a bit, he cleared his throat and said, "Ladies, gentlemen of the Solar System Fine Wines Society, I thank you for this honor. I must also thank my sons, Robert and Jean-Luc—stand, boys."

A spotlight found their table, and the two stood and received a round of applause. As they sat again, Maurice said, "I have no long speech, but I would like to say that this wonderful award only shows that one does not need a replicator, or any clanking machinery, to produce a fine vintage. Automation has no heart. A device of metal and wires is no substitute for the hard, honest labor of people who know and love their land and who understand their business. Thank you for this great honor. I hope Chateau Picard will continue to be worthy of it." He waved to the applauding audience, then made his way back through a forest of well-wishers to the table.

"Congratulations, Father!" said Robert. He sounded as delighted as Maurice looked.

"A wonderful achievement, dear," Yvette said, kissing her husband on the cheek.

"I'm pleased for you," Jean-Luc murmured. Maurice gave him a keen look but said nothing. Two figures wound between the tables, and when they came close enough, Jean-Luc saw that they were his friend Louis and Louis's father, Henri.

"Well, now I know one famous man," Henri said, offering Maurice a hearty handshake. "I'm truly happy for you, my friend. In fact, I'm glad I let Louis talk me into coming here—I hate dressing in these ridiculous costumes." Although Henri was a physician, he had a bluff,

47

informal manner and an infectious laugh. "Well, Louis, are you going to stand there silent?"

"No, sir," Louis said, grinning. "Congratulations, Monsieur Picard." He turned to Jean-Luc. "Things seem to be breaking up. Care to go for a walk with me?"

Jean-Luc looked at his father. Maurice nodded, and Jean-Luc rose from his place. "Here, Dr. Blanchard," he said. "Take my chair. I'm sure you and Father want to talk."

After the crowded hall, the street outside felt cool and looked deserted. Jean-Luc tugged at his tie, loosening it. "Don't," teased Louis. "You'll spoil your dashing good looks."

"I'm with your father," Jean-Luc retorted. "A lot of old-fashioned foolishness, this formal dress."

"Ah, well, you have to suffer to be handsome, you know." They strolled toward the river. Paris, the City of Light, blazed brightly this June evening. After a few steps Louis asked, "Have you done it yet?"

"I haven't tested for Starfleet Academy, if that's what you mean. The July testing period was the first one open. I'm down for that. Now if I can only find some excuse to slip away from home for a week—"

"Oh, a poor schemer like you will never be able to do that," Louis said, a light edge of sarcasm in his voice. "Well, you may be interested to know that Misty and Kim Bloom will be in town tomorrow. Misty's flying in from Melbourne tonight, and the three of us are going to meet for lunch to plan our cycle tour. Care to join us?"

"Sure," Jean-Luc said, his mind on other things.

"It will be a late lunch," warned Louis. "Misty will

want to sleep later after her trip. Shall we say two o'clock?"

"Fine."

"At the Café Robillard." After a pause Louis said, "We expect to have fried butter bugs and caterpillar pudding. Maybe top it all off with mud pies."

Jean-Luc stopped and turned, startled. "What? What are you talking about?"

"I'm talking about the Café Robillard," Louis returned. "I just wasn't sure you were listening."

"Sorry. I was thinking of something else. Yes, I know the place. I'll be there a little before two." The Seine passed under them as they crossed an ancient arched stone bridge. The two friends paused halfway across to look at the river. The water below was black, but it reflected the shimmering glow of street lamps, the occasional streak of a meteor trail. "I look forward to tomorrow," Jean-Luc said, "but for right now, come with me over to our hotel. Father and Mother have a round of parties to make. They won't be coming back for hours, and I don't want to sit around bored and alone. It's early, and we can play a few hands of cards."

"Not that horrible game you tried to teach me last month, I hope? I can't even remember what it was called."

"Six-pack bezique," Jean-Luc said. "Yes, a few hands would be fun. Are you prepared to lose, Louis?"

Louis looked up into the dark night sky, where only a few stars shone, their light dimmed by the lights of Paris. "Oh, you fates," he moaned in mock exasperation. "Why did you make me the best friend of a cardsharp?"

* * *

Lunch the next day was very pleasant. Misty Bloom was very nearly a duplicate of her sister, only with more freckles. She didn't talk as much, either, but she had a quick wit and a devastating way of taking the wind out of Louis's sails when he got too lively.

"You would have loved Medlab," Kim said to her sister. "It's practically a city in the sea."

"Sounds like that ancient poem," Misty said. "Who wrote it? Poe?"

"I thought he was a horror writer," Louis said. "Believe me, there's nothing horrible about Medlab."

"Except swimming down to it," Jean-Luc said as he finished the last bite of a delicious French pastry. "Misty, Louis here is perfectly equipped to be a great marine scientist except for one small thing. He swims like a brick!"

Louis laughed and shrugged. "What can I say? It's true. But you know, that doesn't seem to matter. I've found the place where I belong."

"At the bottom of the ocean?" asked Misty with an encouraging smile.

"That's where it happens to be," Louis replied, his voice suddenly serious. "Oh, I might wish it were elsewhere, but it isn't. And if I have to swim down to the bottom to find my dream, why then, I'll swim. It's worth it, you know."

Misty touched his hand. "I know," she said. "I feel the same way. The first time I opened a computer and saw the positronic circuits humming away, I fell in love. Kim here thinks I'm crazy to go into some indoor field.

She'd rather be out on the range any day. But I agree with you. The dream's worth it."

Kim shook her head. "When did I ever say you were crazy?" She turned to Jean-Luc. "When we were kids, Misty was the one who learned to ride a horse, shear a sheep, and plow a furrow. I always wanted to be inside then. But I supposed we've traded places this last year. Now I want to be an ecologist, and she's the one stuck indoors."

Louis filled all their glasses from a large green bottle of sparkling water. "Well, we all have dreams to chase," he said. "A toast: May we all catch our dreams one fine day!"

They clinked glasses, but Jean-Luc drank to the toast without a smile.

Later, when Louis proposed taking the girls on a tour of the historic sites of Paris, Jean-Luc begged off. Louis didn't seem to mind. He strolled away between the two sisters, both of them talking a hundred kilometers a second.

Jean-Luc watched them go. He was thoughtful and a little afraid. That morning his father had spoken about his own plans for the next few weeks, and to Jean-Luc's delight, they gave him exactly the opening he had wanted.

Now, if he only dared to chase his dream—

If he only dared.

A few days later Robert and Jean-Luc flew their father into LaBarre, where he would take a connecting shuttle to the London trans-Atlantic transport. He grumbled during the short aircar flight into the city, he grumbled while they checked the time of departure, and he grumbled while they waited for the call to board the shuttle. "Two weeks in California," he growled. "Wonderful. I'll get to visit all sorts of vineyards that are as automated as factories!"

"Cheer up, Father," Robert said with a grin. "As the winner of the Prix du Soleil, you're supposed to give seminars for other winegrowers. Who knows? You might even teach them a thing or two."

"Not that bunch of replicating, machine-crazy technologists," retorted Maurice. "I know their type too well. They never have time to do things properly. To them farming is all glitter and machinery, and no heart. Some of them think that the swill they get from replicators is just as good as fine vintage port." He sighed. "Well, Jean-Luc, at least this will be good practice for you. I leave you in charge. All decisions are in your hands. This will help you see what life will be like when your brother deserts us."

A chime sounded, and Robert said, "That's the shuttle. You'd better go."

"Well, goodbye. Take care of everything for me."

"Don't worry," Jean-Luc said. *"Bon voyage."*

Maurice snorted and stumped away, carrying his two suitcases. Robert and Jean-Luc didn't talk until Robert started the aircar and lifted off from the landing lot. "A message came for you this morning," he said, his voice emotionless. "Lucky for you I'm the one who took it. You're to report to the European Testing Center in three days."

"Thank you," Jean-Luc said. He stared out the window at the countryside below, hedgerows and cultivated fields and the occasional cottage.

"Don't thank me!" snapped Robert. "Don't you know what you're doing to all of us?"

"Robert, I—"

"This will break Father's heart. You're the genius of the family. You should be able to understand something simple like that." Robert slowed the aircar to a crawl. Ordinarily Chateau Picard was only a two-minute trip to or from LaBarre, but Robert was stretching it out because he obviously had something to say. "Jean-Luc, it's you he wants to run the vineyard, not me. What if you pass your stupid tests?"

"I will pass," Jean-Luc said. "I didn't pass the last time because of Father."

"What? How dare you blame him? He gave you permission to take the tests." Robert's voice rose in anger, shook with fury. He took a couple of deep breaths and then added sullenly, "That's a lot more than he would have done for me."

Jean-Luc shook his head. "You don't understand. Yes, he gave me permission to test for Starfleet Academy, but he made it clear that he didn't want me to pass. All my life I've done everything to please him. Well, that should be enough. Just this once I'm going to do something to please myself instead."

"And you don't care about Father?"

"Of course I care about him," snapped Jean-Luc. "But it's my life, not his. I have to do this, Robert, whether it hurts Father or—" He broke off and turned to look at Robert. "Or you," he added quietly. "I'm sorry."

"I wondered when you'd think of that." Robert's voice held a sneer. "Yes, of course. I've only waited five years for my chance to win a diploma, to study off-world. If you take the tests and pass, Father will never let me go to Alkalurops. Congratulations, little bother. You're making a fine mess for everyone else in the family."

"I don't intend to," Jean-Luc said. He felt miserable, uncertain, and childish. "You have a right to be upset with me, Robert, but remember that you can choose your own path just as I have to choose mine."

"Oh, that would be just wonderful, wouldn't it? For both of a man's sons to turn against him?"

"No!" objected Jean-Luc. "It isn't like that at all. I'm not turning against Father. He's wrong about me, that's all. I'd never be happy here, Robert, not like you. You and Father are just alike. You love the vineyard, the warmth of the sun, the sweetness of the rain. Sometimes I think you value the grapes and the wine more than you do your own flesh and blood. I'm not like you, and I'm not like him. For whatever it's worth, Robert, I must do what I'm called to do."

"And you hear a different call."

"Yes," Jean-Luc agreed. "I hear a different call."

Robert sped the aircar up again, and in a moment they were gliding in toward their own garage, behind the chateau. "I don't want to talk about this again," Robert said coldly. "You do whatever you have to, Jean-Luc. I can never forgive you for what you're doing to Father, that's all."

Jean-Luc didn't answer. When the aircar landed, he got out and went straight to his room to study. He did not come down for dinner, nor for breakfast the next day. His mother took him a tray at noon, and again that night and the next morning. It was as if she knew all along that Jean-Luc would try again. He didn't need to say anything. She just understood. She sat on the foot of his bed as he ate his breakfast at his desk.

His room seemed strange to him now, the room of a much younger Jean-Luc. The carefully built model ships in bottles might as well have been kindergarten toys. "The worst of it is," he said, picking up his model of the original *Starship Enterprise,* "is that no matter what I do, I let someone down—Father, Robert, myself."

His mother came to stand beside him and brushed his

55

hair into place. "You don't know everything about your father," she said softly. "Would it surprise you to know that Maurice and your grandfather quarreled over the vineyard? Not once, but many times?"

Jean-Luc blinked. "I didn't know that. What was the problem between them?"

With a smile Yvette said, "The problem was that Maurice was his father's son—just as you are Maurice's son. Oh, Jean-Luc, you don't know how very proud he is of you. He never tells you, and sometimes I think he keeps it a secret even from himself. But he is proud of you, and part of his pride is that you are who you are: intelligent, eager to succeed, and yes, stubborn. I think some part of him would be surprised or even hurt if you did *not* test again for Starfleet Academy."

Jean-Luc sighed and put down the model starship. "It will be a very small part," he said ruefully. "Most of him will want to kick me to the moon."

"Well, perhaps not that far," his mother said, and they both had a fit of giggling.

That made him feel somewhat better, but he kept to his room all that day, packing and reading. When he came out again, he carried his suitcase. He looked so woebegone that his mother took him quietly aside to speak to him about his decision. "If you think this is best," she said with a smile, "you must go through with it. Not many decisions are easy, Jean-Luc. This one is at least clear."

"I feel trapped," Jean-Luc admitted.

The feeling did not leave him as his mother flew him into Paris in the aircar. Their goodbyes were brief.

Jean-Luc joined a loose gang of other young men and woman walking toward the complex of shining white stone and glass buildings. It looked as if it might be the headquarters of a small company or the campus of a minor technological college.

It was neither. Jean-Luc passed beneath an arch with lettering on it that read STARFLEET ACADEMY: EUROPEAN TESTING CENTER.

He took a deep breath. Whatever happened now, it was too late to back out. He had to see it through.

CHAPTER

6

Engineering. Command. Psychology.

As he lay in bed that night, trying to sleep, the words swirled around in Jean-Luc's mind like three birds of prey ready to swoop in for the kill. When he dozed, he could almost feel their cruel shadows passing over him, and he cringed a little.

Engineering. Command. Psychology.

They were his three weak points, or more precisely, two weak points and an absolute unknown. Last year his scores had been respectable in all other fields. It was the fiendishly difficult multidimensional calculus of Cochrane engineering that first tripped him up. A computer helped, but its operator had to know exactly what terms to key in and what equations to set up. Besides accuracy, speed also counted. Jean-Luc had been too cautious last year, pausing to double-check every problem before going on to the next, and he had lost valuable seconds. Ironically, on that test he made only three trivial mistakes in the problems he solved. Unfortunately, he ran out of time with five problems left to go and with a time score that put him down around the eighty-seventh percentile. That would have been a respectable score in a typical classroom, but Starfleet demanded ninetieth or higher.

Command was even more unpredictable. Last year he had taken the bridge of a medium-sized reconnaisance starship for a closeup survey of a class-M planet, circa 2220, back when the Federation was at war or on the verge of war with a half dozen different alien races. Of course, the bridge had been only a simulation on a holodeck, and the planet was just imaginary. Even most of his crew had been simulated, except for his first officer, a gray-haired Starfleet veteran, and a cool Vulcan lieutenant who observed and later explained in icy detail every mistake she caught him in. And there had been many, because in the middle of the survey a Klingon warship had suddenly appeared.

Its commander claimed the planet for his empire, warned the Earth ship away, then opened fire without giving Jean-Luc the opportunity of replying. Jean-Luc tried to fight back, but he had neglected to check the status of his weapons. In simulation at least, the Klingons defeated him and his crew.

The Command test would be different this year, he knew, but there was no way to predict what it might be. He could only study Starfleet history and hope that whatever simulation he faced might have some basis in past Starfleet actions.

And then the unknown: the psychology test.

It was different for everyone, he had heard. The psychology test evaluated a candidate's ability to handle extreme stress. The catch was that the Academy could do that in a number of different ways. Jean-Luc had signed a release, for example, that allowed a Betazoid to monitor his thought and emotion patterns. Betazoids were all somewhat telepathic. All of them could read emotions, and some could literally read minds. It could be that a Betazoid would simply listen in to Jean-Luc's fears and thoughts and then give him a score.

Or, for some, the psych test was a maddening examination, full of picky detail, set at a speed barely beyond their ability to respond. The frustration would build and build until the candidate reacted to it—by getting angry, by freezing up, by giving in to despair. And there were even more elaborate and scary ways of measuring psychological fitness. This was the test that frightened everyone.

Engineering. Command. Psychology.

Jean-Luc woke with a start the next morning. Early sunlight slanted through the dorm window. He had fallen asleep with his head on his desk, his cheek resting on a computer padd displaying a physics text on containment fields and Jeffries arrays. He checked the time. It was just sunup, and he still had time to get in a run. That, he thought, was one of his downfalls last year—he had been physically tense, and this year he planned to work out his tension with a morning run before the tests began. He rose stiffly from the chair, stretched, and hurried to unpack his running shorts and shoes.

In an hour he would be due at breakfast, and then he had the literary/philosophical essay to write. He had already decided to do his essay on the work of John Devlin, a twentieth-century poet and writer. Devlin's books *Where Youth and Laughter Go* and *When Duty Whispers Low* had changed a lot of Jean-Luc's ideas regarding the glory of war. Devlin, he decided, would have approved of Starfleet's gradual evolution from a military service to one devoted to the gaining of scientific knowledge.

Jean-Luc paused in the act of pulling on his right running shoe. Something was tucked into the toe. He shook it out into his hand. It was a small object wrapped in white paper, and when he unfolded the paper, he saw it bore lines of writing. It was a brief note from his brother:

Dear Jean-Luc,
 They used to think this brought good luck. Knowing you, you will not need any. But I can't let you go off to be tested without giving you a token of apology or without wishing you the best success.
                                        Your stubborn brother,
                                                    Robert

Robert had wrapped the note around a small silver medallion. Jean-Luc's throat tightened a little. He recognized the gift as an ancient Saint Christopher's medal, a token that had been in the Picard family for generations.

It had accompanied one of Jean-Luc's remote ancestors on a crusade to Jerusalem and back, and later it had gone into space with a great-great grandfather who helped to settle Mars. Maurice had given the medal to Robert when his eldest son graduated from high school—and now here it was in Jean-Luc's hand. He smiled and put the Saint Christopher's medal in a drawer. It wouldn't do any harm to wear it to the tests, he thought, although he certainly wasn't going to rely on a small piece of jewelry for the results. And he certainly wasn't going to risk losing a family heirloom by wearing it while he ran.

He went out into a cool, clear morning and ran for five kilometers, an easy distance and a relaxed pace. Then he showered and dressed quickly. He was halfway out the door when he remembered the Saint Christopher's medal. With a smile, he grabbed it and slipped it on. *It couldn't hurt,* he thought with a shrug as he hurried from his room.

He ate breakfast in the commissary with the other hopeful candidates, all of them human except for Molvantar, a willowy, blue-skinned Andorian, the son of the Andorian consul for Europe. They chatted with one another in high, nervous voices about the five days of testing ahead.

"They say that the competition is really fierce this time around," said red-haired Sandy McCannon, a girl who had a frightening command of engineering skills. "Oh, why didn't I go to the first testing cycle?"

Jan Helmer, a lanky blond boy with a devil-may-care grin and a habit of working out complex navigation problems on paper napkins, said, "You know the answer to that, Sandy. Like all the rest of us, you had a point or two you had to study. You'll pass the engineering test with no problem—but what about literature? What about history? What about command?"

"You did not mention navigation," Molvantar murmured, his antennae twitching. "That is my greatest worry. My father has hired tutors and I've logged weeks of computer time, but I still don't understand all the concepts."

"All of us are dreading something," Jan said. He raised an eyebrow at Jean-Luc. "What are you afraid of, Frenchy?"

With an easy smile Jean-Luc said, "Please don't call me that, Mr. Helmer. I have a name."

"Sorry, Monsieur Picard. What are you afraid of?"

"No one thing," Jean-Luc said and turned his attention back to his breakfast crepe. His boastful claim was true, in a way. He wasn't afraid of any *one* thing. He was afraid of practically everything, every test that could trip him up, keep him out, make him fail.

As soon as breakfast ended, an ensign herded the candidates into a small lecture room. The room had two hundred seats in it, and the candidates filled not even half of them. Jean-Luc guessed that ninety students from Europe, Asia, and the African Confederation were contending for the appointments to the Academy. Since this was the last testing period of the year, most of the Academy's new cadets had already received their acceptances. Jean-Luc took a deep breath and wondered how many of the students in the room would make the final cut.

He did not have long to wonder. A gray-haired woman in the uniform of a Starfleet Commander walked out onto the stage and to a lectern. "Good morning," she said, looking out at them. "I trust you all had pleasant journeys to the testing center and a good night's sleep last night. I assure you, you will need it."

A few people giggled nervously. The woman did not pause. "I am Commander Cynthia Luttrell, retired. However, as many Starfleet veterans discover, it is not so easy to retire from Starfleet. Rather than enjoying the sun and surf at Paradise Island on Walzinger's Planet, I have accepted an appointment here as the director of Academy testing, European division."

She seemed to look directly at Jean-Luc with a cool, level gaze. "This morning I have reviewed the applications and the vacancies at Starfleet. As it happens, this year has seen a wave of young Vulcan applicants to the Academy."

Someone groaned. Jean-Luc fought back a grin. It was true that Vulcans had formidable minds, but they weren't *that* good—and not that numerous. Commander Luttrell continued: "Added to the number of Vulcan applicants, we have the fact that the Academy had a good selection of candidates from the previous five testing cycles. All of this is just my way of telling you that competition will be especially stringent. Last year our center sent eight cadets to Starfleet from the July testing cycle. This year we will be able to send only one."

A wave of sighs and moans swept through the assembly hall. Jean-Luc felt his heart sink. His chance had suddenly dwindled from practically one in ten to one in ninety. But then so had everyone else's, as the dismayed expressions of the students showed.

"I won't say anything more to discourage you," Commander Luttrell concluded. "The testing will begin in half an hour. Be on time for all the tests. My assistant will answer any last-minute questions you may have." She suddenly smiled, a radiant smile that made her lined face look young and girlish. "For what it's worth, candidates, I envy you. Good luck to you all, and keep your hopes on the stars."

A young ensign took over, answering a few silly questions with an absolutely straight face—after all, Jean-Luc thought, what did it matter if one used the old-fashioned imprimis computer padd instead of the newer models? Then it was time for the first examination. The candidates split up into smaller groups for that. Jean-Luc and fourteen others, including Sandy McCannon, wrote essays. Jean-Luc had guessed well, because one of the topics was "Discuss a work of literature from the twenty-second century or earlier that substantially altered your view of modern society." He was able to adapt the Devlin topic handily.

For an hour he worked at the essay, pausing occasionally to access library holdings with his computer padd. He retrieved articles and essays about Devlin, even facsimiles of Devlin's original poetry manuscripts. He had a draft of the essay finished in ninety minutes, and thirty minutes remained for him to revise and polish it. He felt confident that he had done a good job when the ensign overseeing the essays called time and locked the essays in on his own computer padd. Jean-Luc looked over at Sandy and felt startled to see her red-faced and biting her lip.

"What's wrong?" he asked her.

She shrugged. "I don't think I did very well on that. Writing is not my strong point. How about you?"

"I think I did all right," Jean-Luc said. "Don't worry. When we finish the engineering tests, you'll be the happy one and I'll be a wreck."

She gave him a weak smile, and they moved along to the advanced Cochrane mathematics examination. Jean-Luc settled in at a terminal, one of ten, with Sandy beside him. The first question appeared: "Given a starship propelled by two standard warp field nacelles operating at 50 percent capacity, beginning from a sublight speed of $.1c$ relative to its destination D, calculate the time T

required for the warp field energy to reach the milicoch-rane output necessary to move the vessel along the *c* boundary at precisely the speed of light."

Sandy began furious computations, but Jean-Luc immediately keyed in his response: zero. It was a trick question. Starships *never* traveled at precisely the speed of light. They had to move either slower or faster than *c*—otherwise, there would be no boundary, and Planck physics would make no sense. Sandy belatedly realized this. Jean-Luc was halfway through the second question when he heard her grunt of self-directed anger.

At last they both finished, each feeling reasonably sure of a good score—though Jean-Luc had a nasty, nagging dread that he had overlooked something, that he had failed again. By now the other candidates were looking frazzled and exhausted. Jean-Luc began to feel a little flicker of hope. Maybe he wouldn't disgrace himself completely. In fact, he began to suspect there might be a possibility of his passing the exams. After all, he realized suddenly, he'd just passed the one test that had tripped him up last year! The engineering test would take all afternoon. If only he could weather that one, he thought, then the next ones might not be as bad as he feared.

They broke for lunch, and since he had ninety minutes, Jean-Luc decided to go into Paris for a meal away from the hectic pace of the testing center. He had just settled in at a sidewalk café when his computer padd blipped. He put it in communication mode and heard Louis's cheerful voice: "Hello, Jean-Luc! Are you in town?"

"Yes," Jean-Luc said, grinning. "You knew I'd be test-

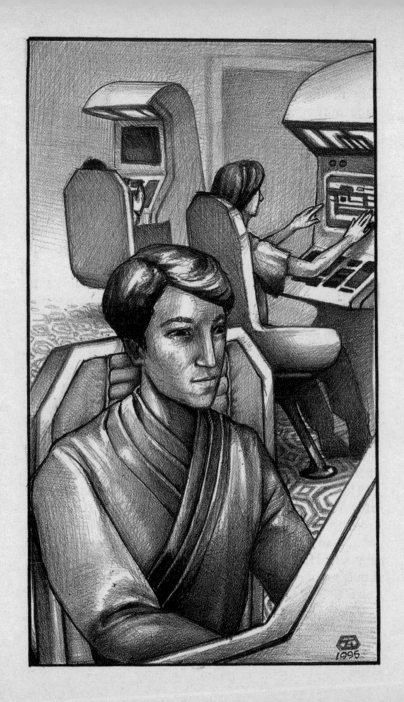

ing for Starfleet again. Except right now I'm having lunch at the Four Candles."

"I'm only a few blocks away! Stay put, Jean-Luc, and we'll join you in ten minutes."

"We?" Jean-Luc asked, but Louis had already broken the connection. As Jean-Luc ordered his lunch, he wondered who "we" would turn out to be.

He didn't wonder very long. Louis came rattling over the cobblestone street on a bike, with Kim Bloom on his right and Misty on his left. All three looked tan and fit, and they clattered their bikes right up to Jean-Luc's table.

"Hello," he said, delighted to see them. "Have some lunch."

"We've eaten, thanks," Louis said. He put one arm around Kim's waist, the other around her sister's. Jean-Luc could not help giving his friend a roguish grin. He had warned Louis about what might happen!

"How are your tests going?" Kim asked as she pulled away from Louis and parked her bike.

Jean-Luc shrugged. "No decision either way, yet. Maybe you'll bring me luck." They settled in for mineral water and chitchat. Jean-Luc ate his lunch while both Kim and Misty stole little bites of his shrimp salad. An hour flew by, with Jean-Luc feeling not exactly jealous but a little excluded. Louis clearly enjoyed being the center of both Misty's and Kim's attention, and he was full of their bike trip. They had already toured Paris and the countryside to the north, and they were setting out this afternoon for a long excursion southward into Provence.

"Be careful," Jean-Luc warned him. "You cycle about

as well as you swim. The way you wobbled along down the street, I thought you were about to fall off and break an arm."

"They're teaching me to be a better cyclist," Louis said. "Did you know Misty won her town's cycling competition last year?"

"Yes, Kim told me twice," Jean-Luc said with a smile. "Well, I've got to get back to the testing center. Have a good trip. Kim, Misty, take care of this clumsy fellow."

"We will," Kim said with a laugh. "And you have wonderful luck on your exams."

They rode away, and Jean-Luc watched them. He had never seen Louis so happy, and he was heartily glad for his friend. At the same time he felt a little pang of doubt. In a way he would like to be like Louis, spending time just having fun. It had been a hard year, and the deceptions and secrecy had made it all the harder. If only he could be as carefree as his friends, just for a few days, he thought he would be supremely happy.

However, he had an appointment with a test supervisor in twenty minutes. He summoned an aircar and rode back to the testing center, worrying again about engineering, command, and psychology.

CHAPTER

7

The room was made of perfectly black squares, outlined by the gold lines of the holoconductors. Jean-Luc stood in the center and waited for something to happen. This was a holodeck, similar to those used on Federation starships for training and for recreation. It was capable of creating vivid three-dimensional illusions of reality, so real that you could touch and smell the images as well as see and hear them.

Jean-Luc drew a deep breath. It was only the third day of testing, and already the competition had dwindled from eighty-nine other hopefuls to just thirty-one. Sandy had washed out on the literary essay, as she had feared, and left with a wry, "Well, there's always next year." The Andorian had vanished, too, although Jean-Luc did not know what had tripped him up. His own testing group was down by more than half. From the fifteen they had started with, only seven remained. Well, no matter what happened, he had made it at least as far this year as he had the previous one—and he felt a lot better about his chances this time around.

Jean-Luc glanced down at his uniform and nervously tugged the tunic as if to straighten it. The style gave him a clue or two about the command test. It was an old-fashioned Starfleet outfit. He recognized the insignia as that of a commander, an officer who had not yet earned the permanent rank of captain. A communicator, an impossibly bulky thing almost fifteen centimeters long and twelve broad—nearly as long and wide as his hand!—hung at his belt. Old-fashioned, that was the key. Think, Jean-Luc told himself. What do you know about Starfleet, date approximately 2150–2175?

Well, it was a more military organization than current Starfleet, exploring the universe and coming into contact with hostile aliens. Crews and ships all Earth-based, of course. There had been a war or two, notably with the Romulans. He wondered if—

"Attention, cadet candidate Jean-Luc Picard. Are you receiving me?"

"Yes."

A long pause. Then, patiently, the dehumanized computer voice said, "I remind you to use your communicator, cadet candidate."

Jean-Luc blushed and took the awkward thing from his belt. He flipped it open, extended the primitive subspace antenna, and said, "Yes, I receive you."

"Your assignment for the command test is to take command of a Starfleet probe ship mapping and exploring four class-M planets in Sector Fifteen-G. Your armament consists of three arrays of four pulse-phase laser cannon and a battery of twenty particle torpedoes. Your top speed is warp three point five, and your optimum cruising speed is warp two. Your ship has surveyed three of the four planets in question, finding them life-bearing but without intelligent inhabitants. You have just entered standard orbit around Sigma Oronyx Four. Here is a representation of the planet."

The walls shimmered and seemed to dissolve into the darkness of star-sparkling space. A huge representation of a planet hovered above Jean-Luc, a world of approximately equal parts sea and land, the shallow water a shimmering golden color, the land a vibrant blue-green, studded with enormous jet-black dead volcanoes and streaked with swirls and spirals of cloud. Jean-Luc frowned. He recognized the planet. It was now known as Van Damen's World, with a well-established population, chiefly humans and Bolians. There was something in history about its discovery, though, something that he could not quite remember.

"Computer, I have some questions," Jean-Luc said.

"Ask."

"What is the complement of my ship?"

"You have a crew of twenty-nine. Your first officer is Lieutenant Andrew Chen. Your science officer is Lieutenant Ariadne Korzeniowski. Your weapons officer and chief of security is Lieutenant J. R. Newell."

That did no good, thought Jean-Luc as he made a real

effort to lock the names into his memory. It wouldn't do to fumble for a name at a crucial moment. What was it that his memory was trying to tell him? Perhaps one more question. "Thank you, computer. And what is the name of my vessel?"

"You are commanding the *U.S.S. Ponce de Leon*."

Jean-Luc swallowed hard. He had read about the *Ponce de Leon* weeks ago, in the Xenology library. Now he knew. Oh, yes, indeed, he knew all too well what he was up against.

The *Ponce de Leon* was a byword in Starfleet for a ship in a hopeless position. It all flooded back from his reading now: In the year 2159, during the height of the Romulan-Earth War, the *Ponce de Leon* had blundered into two Romulan destroyers, ships that had been damaged in an earlier battle and that had dropped into orbit here to refit. What resulted was less a fight than an act of annihilation. An under-armed survey vessel with only primitive weapons, the *Ponce de Leon* had been lost with all hands, and only a desperate message, sent by old-fashioned radio, had told the universe of their fate.

"The simulation will begin fifteen seconds from now," the computer said.

The planet schematic faded, but not before Jean-Luc had noted almost absentmindedly that Van Damen's World had three tiny moons orbiting it, hardly larger than moderate-sized asteroids. The fifteen seconds seemed to take a week. Again Jean-Luc nervously tugged at his tunic.

Then the darkness shimmered into shape and form. He was standing behind three officers in an incredibly

cramped command compartment. Something told him
that the windows in front of him were real windows and
not viewscreens. Through them he could see the rounded
silver nose of the *Ponce de Leon,* and beyond that the
planet itself, slowly rotating.

"Standard orbit, sir," said the woman to his left.

"Thank you, Lieutenant Korzeniowski." Jean-Luc
took a deep breath. No Romulans were in sight, so he
couldn't order an alert. He'd have to justify it later.
"You may commence your survey of the planet."

"Aye-aye, sir."

For a few moments they cruised in silence. Jean-Luc
was trying to deal with the weird feeling that he was
playing a game, as he had often done when he was just
a kid. His officers were all older than he was, by ten

years or more. He wondered how they saw him, and then immediately felt foolish. They weren't even real. They were only holographic illusions that the computer generated.

And yet it all *seemed* real. The air had the sharp scent of metal and electricity, and under that the stuffy odor that was a little like that of a locker room. It was a tight little compartment, and people manned it twenty-four hours a day, every day.

"Sir," said Lieutenant Newell, sounding puzzled. "I'm picking up traces of ionized plasma."

"Location?"

The security officer shook his head. "I can't pinpoint it. It's at orbital distance, perhaps five thousand kilometers from the planetary surface. Very diffuse. Perhaps it's some atmospheric reaction. This is a class-F Nine star, more active than our sun."

"Or it could be the trace of a starship impulse engine," Jean-Luc said.

Lieutenant Chen looked over his shoulder, his brown eyes troubled. "Unlikely, sir. Any plasma traces from our early unmanned probes would have dissipated months ago."

Jean-Luc rubbed his chin. "Well, perhaps I'm being overly cautious, but just to be on the safe side, let's change orbit. Number One, put us at the same orbital distance as that small moon ahead. Keep us about a thousand kilometers away from it. We can scan the planetary surface from there just as well as you could from here."

"Our resolution won't be one hundred percent, sir," warned Lieutenant Korzeniowski.

"No, but it will be close enough. We'll reserve anything interesting or puzzling for a closer look during the next stage of the survey. Number One, you have my orders."

"Aye-aye, sir."

It was coming back, all of it. The *Ponce de Leon* was such a compact ship that the First Officer also served as helmsman. Chen laboriously keyed in instructions—imagine not being able just to tell the computer what you wanted it to do! The ship responded, the impulse engines coming on-line to boost their trajectory higher, closer to the small tumbling chunk of rock that was Van Damen's World's lowest moon. They slipped into the new orbit. Jean-Luc gazed out at the irregular speck of moon. "Can we magnify that fifty times?" he asked.

"Aye-aye, sir." Lieutenant Korzeniowski manipulated a board of instruments, and a representation of the moon came up on a display screen at her science station.

Jean-Luc leaned in close. It was a dark red body, pocked with craters and crisscrossed by stress fractures. "What is the composition of that, Lieutenant?" he asked.

"Sir, I'm scanning the surface of the planet at the moment. If it could wait—"

"I'm afraid it can't."

The science officer grunted with ill-concealed displeasure and recalibrated one of her instruments. "I'm sounding it with a laser probe," she said. "Spectroscopic

77

analysis will take about half a minute." After a pause she added, "Sir."

"How about that plasma trace?" Jean-Luc asked Lieutenant Newell.

Newell, probably the oldest person on the bridge, shook his head. "I still can't get any kind of fix on it. If a spacecraft has been using its impulse engines around here, it hasn't been in the past couple of weeks."

"I still think it's probably natural ionization," muttered Lieutenant Korzeniowski. "Spectroscopic results coming in. Sir, the moon consists of various mineral ores, chiefly iron, with smaller proportions of copper, zinc, and lead. These account for approximately fifty percent of its mass. The remainder is common silicate and carbonaceous rock."

"Noted, Lieutenant."

"May I redirect my sensors to the planet, sir?"

"Yes."

"Just another moon," she muttered.

"Uh-oh," Newell said. "Sir? We've got company."

Jean-Luc's hands were sweating. "Where away?" he asked, slipping into the naval jargon he had so often read in stories of adventure. "I mean, bearing and mark?"

"Bearing one-seven-seven, mark negative twenty-one."

Behind and below them, ideally spotted for a sneak attack. "How far?"

"Four hundred thousand kilometers, closing fast."

"Lieutenant Chen, take her around that moon. Make it look as if we're running for cover. But the second Lieutenant Newell says we're out of scanner range, I want you to put the *Ponce de Leon* into as tight a turn as she can stand. We'll slingshot around the moon and get a look at who's so interested in us."

"Aye-aye, Captain," said both lieutenants at once.

The *Ponce de Leon* leaped forward, the movement translating itself as a sickening lurch. *The inertial damping systems had not been perfect back in 2159,* Jean-Luc thought. Well, neither were the Romulan warships of that year. Although they used fearsome nuclear weapons, the Romulan craft didn't even have warp drive. Of course, that had not stopped them from devastating over a hundred warp-equipped Earth vessels.

"Executing turn, sir," said Chen.

The centripetal force made it hard for Jean-Luc to stand. He realized his command chair was right behind him. He settled into it, but he was leaning forward, his eyes on the streaking stars visible through the forward windows. The planet flashed past, a blur of green and blue and white, and then the view steadied. "There," Jean-Luc said. "A Romulan. Shields up. Red alert. Mr. Newell, ready all weapons."

The computer hooted a klaxon warning as the weapons officer brought his banks of pulsed-phased laser cannon and torpedo tubes on-line. Newell grunted. "Very far from home, aren't they? What are they doing here?"

"Several Romulans were unaccounted for at the Battle of the Flame Nebula, about half a light-year from here," Chen responded. "This one's had just about enough time to get this far from the site of the battle, although it's not heading toward Romulan space. It might have been damaged and—"

"Belay the talk," Jean-Luc said. "Stop the red-alert signal—if our people don't know we're on alert now, they never will. Lieutenant Korzeniowski, hail the Romulan."

"Aye, sir." Lieutenant Korzeniowski's voice was tight, tense. "Hailing. Sir, they're responding."

"Put them on."

"Sir, they are on."

Jean-Luc grimaced. Right. In the old days there had been no video displays for subspace communication between different star-faring races. The technology had not been able to handle alien signals efficiently then. "Romulan vessel," said Jean-Luc, hoping his voice wasn't shaking too much. "This is the captain of the Earth vessel *Ponce de Leon,* on a peaceful survey mission. What is your intention?"

"Sir, they've hove to," muttered Newell.

A pause, and then a strange voice crackled over the communicator, all of its personality lost because of the primitive universal translator. "Captain of the *Ponce de Leon,* this is Romulan captain Sharak. Our vessel was disabled in warfare. We have undertaken repairs."

Jean-Luc gripped the arms of his command chair. "Well, Captain Sharak, my vessel is not primarily a ship of war. May I suggest a truce?"

Newell looked sharply at him. Romulans were not known for accepting truces.

The Romulan's voice came back at once: "We have completed repairs, Earth captain. If you will permit us, we will leave under full impulse power for Romulan

81

space within the next ten of your minutes. You will wish to report our presence here to your superiors. We acknowledge your responsibility to do so, but as a gesture of good faith, we ask that you make your initial report by radio instead of by subspace communication."

"Understood and granted."

"Thank you, Captain."

Lieutenant Korzeniowski said, "They've broken off communication, sir."

"Sir!" said Newell. "You can't believe them. No one can trust a Romulan."

"Don't be too sure that I do trust them, Lieutenant. Maintain a full scan. Move us back to within five hundred kilometers of that moon, but let it seem as though we're drifting. Mr. Newell, target the moon with a particle torpedo."

"Target—the *moon,* sir?" asked the incredulous Newell.

"That was my order. Be ready to fire instantly when I give the word. Mr. Chen, I will want warp one for precisely one second, at my command."

Lieutenant Korzeniowski had the Romulan craft on her display screen. It was a compact ship of war, with great black splotches on its external plates, the marks of pulsed-phase lasers. The ship was making a slow yawing revolution, as if about to leave planetary orbit on a trajectory for Galactic north. Beyond it the planet rotated peacefully.

"Sir!" yelled Newell. "A second ship has just come

from behind the planet. It's heading straight for us at high impulse speed!"

"The first ship has put shields up. They're turning to fire!" shouted Chen.

"Steady," said Jean-Luc. "Steady." He was ready for a tremendous gamble. For him, this was no longer a game.

Now he was playing for keeps.

CHAPTER

8

"Steady," Jean-Luc ordered, his eyes narrowing as the second Romulan vessel hurtled directly toward them. "Steady."

"The first ship's locked on to us!" shouted Newell. "They're about to open fire!"

"Mr. Newell, fire aft torpedo at the moon! Mr. Chen, I want warp one . . ." Jean-Luc drew the word out. There! A fiery, twinkling projectile left the nearer Romulan! "Now!" shouted Jean-Luc.

A moment's disorientation, and then the ship dropped out of warp a quarter of a million kilometers from where it had been. "Turn us 180 degrees," Jean-Luc commanded. "Bring the ship to bear on the moon."

From here, a light-second away, the shrunken moon

was just a bright, irregular blotch against the darkness of space. Suddenly it flared a hundred times brighter than it had shone before. "Our torpedo," said Newell. "But it won't destroy a whole moon."

"It isn't meant to," Jean-Luc said quietly. "Mr. Chen, take us in at full impulse power. Mr. Newell, prepare to target the first Romulan we encounter."

The ship surged forward. The glowing debris of the explosion swelled in the forward windows. A bright dart-like object, one of the Romulans, appeared low and to the left. Chen changed course to bring them right aft of the alien ship. "Fire as soon as we're within range, Mr. Newell. Full group of particle torpedoes."

"Their rear shields are down!" Lieutenant Korzeniowski yelled in surprise. "They've thrown all power to the forward shields. They're wide open!"

"Torpedoes away!" shouted Newell at almost the same moment. A heartbeat later four bright sparks appeared, converging on the delta-strutted form of the Romulan.

"They're raising their shields!" Lieutenant Korzeniowski's voice had gone high-pitched in her excitement. "Too late! One torpedo is through—"

An explosion flared from the Romulan vessel, and then immediately three more erupted. "Their drive is overloading," reported Lieutenant Korzeniowski.

"Veer away," ordered Jean-Luc.

An instant later the Romulan ship became a second sun, an expanding globe of radiation and hot gas. "Target the second ship."

"It's turning to face us," Korzeniowski reported.

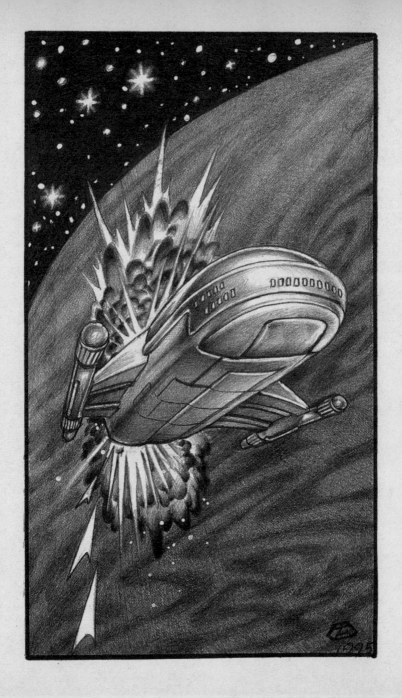

"Torpedoes away," said Newell.

"They can't raise full shields. They must really have taken severe damage." Korzeniowski stared intently at her display screen. "There go the torpedoes. First impacted on the shields. There's the second—third's through! And the fourth!"

The Romulan vessel rocked in space. The enemy had not managed to get off a shot. The ship began to tumble in its orbit, sparks and jets of gas spewing from its forward section. "Sir, they're hailing us," said Korzeniowski, her voice now trembling with reaction.

Jean-Luc realized he had been holding his breath. He let it out slowly and tried to make his voice deep and authoritative: "Put them on, Lieutenant."

The primitive universal translator's voice was toneless, but the words bore their own pain: "We are completely disabled, Earth Captain. Congratulations on your ruse."

"How many do you have aboard?" Jean-Luc asked. "We will take you all on as prisoners of war."

"I think not, Captain. Romulans do not capitulate. We who are about to die salute you."

"Sir," said Korzeniowski, "they're deliberately overloading their fusion core."

"Back us away," Jean-Luc ordered. "Full impulse astern." He swayed as the order was carried out. His gaze remained locked on the forward window. The tumbling, pitching Romulan craft suddenly went the way of its sister ship, detonating with a silent, dazzling blast of deadly energy.

"We won," Lieutenant Chen said, his voice pleased

and puzzled at the same time. "A survey ship against two Romulan war birds, and we won!"

"One of the Romulans was already heavily damaged," Jean-Luc reminded him.

"Still," a new voice said, "it was a great victory."

The *Ponce de Leon*'s command bridge faded away, and Jean-Luc was standing in the holodeck. He was not alone, however. A tall, thin man with a strong nose and penetrating brown eyes had joined him. "Congratulations," the newcomer said. He wore civilian clothing, and he did not introduce himself. "Your solution was unorthodox, but it worked."

"Thank you," Jean-Luc said, feeling suddenly self-conscious, as if an adult had caught him playing some childish game. "I reasoned that the detonation of our torpedo on the surface of the moon would read very much like the explosion of a small ship. The enemy sensors would pick up metal vapors, carbon, everything that a destroyed starship might produce. We were so close to the moon that both Romulans momentarily believed they had destroyed our ship. Also, the Romulans lacked warp-drive technology. I gambled that our sudden complete disappearance when we went to warp one would give them the illusion that our ship had blown up, and evidently it did. That presented us with the edge we needed."

"I see. And how do you feel about your victory?"

"I am happy," Jean-Luc said. "Historically, the *Ponce de Leon* was lost, so I am pleased to have saved it in this recreated encounter."

"No," the stranger said. "You are happy on the surface, but underneath you are troubled."

Jean-Luc's eyes widened. "You are a Betazoid," he said, understanding.

"My name is Trevalion," the stranger said. "Yes, I am a Betazoid. Usually I serve as a counselor at Starfleet Academy, but for this week I am on detached duty here."

Jean-Luc swallowed. Betazoids were all at least partially telepathic. All could read the emotions of others, and some could even understand other people's thoughts. No one could conceal anything from a Betazoid for long.

"Tell me," Trevalion said, "why do you feel uneasy about your victory?"

Jean-Luc bit his lip. The he blurted, "Because I destroyed two vessels, each with a full crew. I acted in the heat of the moment, but now I wonder if it had to be that way. Perhaps I could have reached a compromise somehow. Perhaps I could have saved a great many lives."

"You saved the lives of your own crew," Trevalion pointed out. "Something the original commander of the *Ponce de Leon* could not do. And the others were only Romulans."

Anger seethed inside Jean-Luc. "No one is 'only' anything," he said. "Life is life. If we can't give it back, we shouldn't take it—at least, not lightly."

"You are sincere." It was not a question, but a statement of fact. "Congratulations, Mr. Picard. You scored extremely well on the leadership and decision portions of the command test. I must give you top marks on the judgment scale, too." The tall man placed a fatherly hand on Jean-Luc's shoulder. "Now we will go to my office and talk. Some of your emotions are difficult for you to understand. You will need to come to terms with them."

Reaction set in. That afternoon, following a long session with Trevalion, Jean-Luc was limp with fatigue. He dined with the other candidates, noting that only twelve now remained, with him the thirteenth, the unlucky number, the odd man out. Earlier in the testing period, meals had been a time of teasing and joking. Now the remaining few ate in grim silence. With a shock Jean-Luc realized that he was the only surviving member of his original test group of fifteen. All the others had washed out at some stage of the tests. He was closer to Starfleet Academy than he had ever been in his life.

And tomorrow he had to face the dread psych test. Three of the survivors had already taken it, but from their brief, unhappy comments, the test had been different for each one. Jean-Luc dimly remembered an ancient Earth novel in which the protagonist was sent to face "the worst thing in the world." The worst thing, as it turned out, was whatever the victim feared most, and so it was different for everyone. Jean-Luc had tried for days to decide what he feared most, but without success. He left dinner with the intention of going straight to his room and falling into a dead sleep for twelve hours.

The dormitory halls were silent and empty. Jean-Luc, reeling with weariness, approached his door. It sensed his presence and opened automatically for him. The room was dark, the windows blanking the sunset. "Clear the windows," Jean-Luc ordered, tugging his tunic over his head.

He pulled the garment off and froze. Sitting on his bed, glaring at him, was Maurice Picard.

For half a minute father and son stared at each other. Then Maurice said, "So it is true. I was speaking to a group of recreational farmers in California. One happened to be associated with Starfleet Academy, and he wished me well on my son's application."

Jean-Luc dropped his tunic. "And so you flew straight back to France," he said.

"Of course. And from here I'm going straight back to LaBarre, and you are coming with me."

Jean-Luc pulled a T-shirt over his head. "No, Father," he said. "I have only one test left—"

"You gave your word," Maurice reminded him. "Does that mean nothing to you? I agreed to let you try— once and once only. I thought I made it absolutely clear that—"

"Father," Jean-Luc said, "you don't understand. I'm not cut out to be a winegrower. Robert is, but—"

"Don't tell me about my own sons!" Maurice surged up from the bed, his expression furious. "Robert is a good man, a hard worker, but you—you are the genius of the family! You are the one who could make Picard Vineyards a name known throughout the solar system!"

"You've done that already!" Jean-Luc yelled back. "What else is the Prix du Soleil but a symbol of your fame?"

91

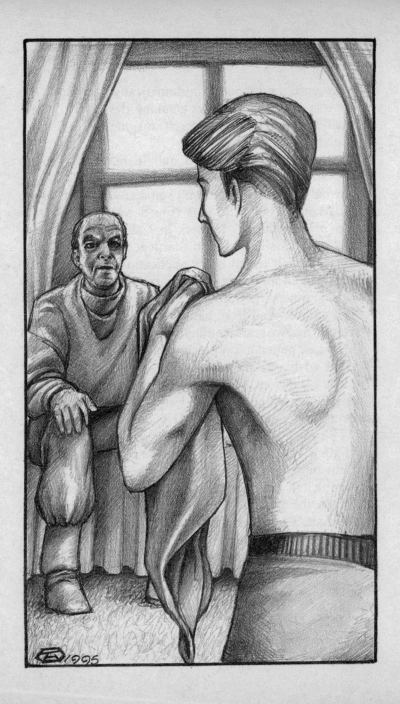

"It has nothing to do with fame," Maurice said, his voice rising. "Fame is simply a measure of how well you do your job, the job that you were born to do, the one that your grandfather was born to do, that I—"

"Father," Jean-Luc interrupted, "I'm not you! Don't you see? Don't you understand? You feel a love for the land deeper than anything else. That's the way I feel about Starfleet. Father, I'm not here because getting into Starfleet Academy is something I want to do. It's something I *have* to do."

"Nonsense! Jean-Luc, why do you hate me so?"

Jean-Luc felt the blood hot in his face. "I don't hate you, Father. I love you."

"You have an odd way of showing it." Maurice rose and came over to his son. He put an arm around Jean-Luc's shoulder. In a coaxing voice he said, "Son, let's forget about all this. You tried once, and you failed. That should tell you something. You will never fail in the vineyard. You have me to teach you, Robert to help you, hundreds of years of tradition behind you. A man should be rooted in his own earth, like a good strong vine, not rattling around in the galaxy. Come home with me."

Jean-Luc pulled away. "I'm not going back, Father," he said, fighting to control his frustration and anger. "I have one remaining test, and if I pass, I'm going to Starfleet Academy."

"And if you fail, you won't come home!" snapped Maurice.

"What?" Jean-Luc stared at him. "Are you kicking me out?"

"I'm washing my hands of you! If you don't come with me now, then you're no son of mine. I won't have a liar and a traitor at my table."

Jean-Luc began, "I've never lied to you—"

"What is all this but a lie?" roared Maurice, sweeping his hand to indicate the testing center, Starfleet Academy, everything. "You didn't even ask my permission! That is the same as a lie. You knew what I wanted, and you deliberately disobeyed. That is treachery. I warn you, Jean-Luc: If you don't come with me this minute, you need never come back at all."

Jean-Luc stood frozen as his father walked to the door. It slipped open, and Maurice stood in the doorway, his face bright red with anger. "Come now, and I'll forget everything. Stay, and you are turning your back on home forever."

Deliberately, Jean-Luc turned away. Behind him he heard the door slide shut.

He was still exhausted, but he no longer felt sleepy.

He wondered if he would ever be able to sleep again.

CHAPTER

9

Somehow Jean-Luc fell into a troubled doze just before dawn. Somehow he slept right through his personal alarm. He woke only when the dormitory speakers blared out the candidates' last warning: "Attention, candidates. You are due at the testing center in fifteen minutes."

Jean-Luc leaped from his bed, dizzy from having only two hours of sleep. He showered and dressed in record time and ran to the testing center on the double, arriving at the last minute and at the end of the line. The others looked as tired as Jean-Luc felt. He was hungry, but there had been no time for breakfast. The candidates stood as Commander Luttrell entered.

She murmured, "As you were." After all had sunk

into their seats again, she said, "Well, candidates, this will be the crucial day for you. As you know, this center will be able to certify only one cadet for Starfleet Academy. You have all done exceptionally well. If you wash out at this stage, I want you to know you have nothing to be ashamed of. Here are the test stations for today." She held up a data padd and read off twelve names, twelve test rooms.

She did not call Jean-Luc's name.

"That's all," she said. "To your test stations, candidates. And good luck to you."

Everyone rose, and the twelve other candidates hurried out, some going to command testing, some to engineering, others to various different sites. Jean-Luc stood uncertainly beside his desk. "Ah—Commander Luttrell," he said in a quiet but anxious voice. "What about me?"

"Ah, yes, candidate Picard." Commander Luttrell gave him a brief, sympathetic smile. "You are to report to Counselor Trevalion's office in one hour." She turned to leave.

"Excuse me, Commander," Jean-Luc said, and she stopped. He cleared his throat. "I don't want to be rude, but why am I seeing Counselor Trevalion? We had a long talk yesterday after the command test."

Commander Luttrell raised an eyebrow. "This isn't about the command test, candidate Picard. I'm sure the counselor will make everything clear to you." When he started to speak again, she cut him off sharply: "One hour, Mr. Picard. Understood?"

"Yes," he said, still feeling bewildered.

The hour gave Jean-Luc time for breakfast, but he

now had little appetite. He had a small cup of hot cocoa and nibbled on a croissant. His father's harsh words kept going through Jean-Luc's mind: *"I'm washing my hands of you."* Did Maurice really mean that? He was an emotional man, and sometimes he overstated his real intentions. But what if his father had been serious? What if Jean-Luc could never return to the vineyard again? What was he to do then?

On the one hand, Jean-Luc had little to worry about. With his grades and school record, any college or university would accept him. But then to think of never seeing his mother or father again, or Robert—it was more than he could bear. Inside his tunic the Saint Christopher's medal dangled on a thin chain he wore around his neck. The cool metal against his chest reminded Jean-Luc of his brother's grudging good wishes. What a pity it would be if Jean-Luc somehow failed to get into Starfleet Academy and still could not return home! And what would his mother say? Yvette Picard could normally calm her husband, but Jean-Luc had never seen Maurice as furious as he had been last night.

With a sigh Jean-Luc drank the last cool dregs of his cocoa, sweet and bitter at the same time, and stared at the ruin of his croissant. He had crumbled the flaky pastry into bits. Some of the crumbs clung to his tunic sleeve. Jean-Luc frowned and dusted them off. It wouldn't do to report to Counselor Trevalion in a messy uniform. And he had only—he checked the time—only forty long minutes in which to wonder and worry.

In the next few minutes Jean-Luc began to think that of all the difficult things he had had to do at the testing center, waiting was the hardest. He mentally reviewed everything he had done over the past four days, the tests, the off-duty times, everything. Nothing seemed to justify his being called to the counselor's office.

Then he began to wonder if the counselor was in charge of the psych test. That might be it—except that other candidates had already been to the psych test in the north wing of the test site. The counselor's office was in the central administrative section. At last, when he still had ten minutes to go, Jean-Luc left the empty commissary and headed for Trevalion's office. It was down the hall from Commander Luttrell's office, and its anteroom had a corner window overlooking a pond and a formal flower garden. The counselor's assistant, a blond young man not much older than Jean-Luc, invited him to have a seat, but Jean-Luc preferred to stand and gaze down at the pond, twenty feet below. Goldfish glided through it, sailing as smoothly as a starship navigated the spaces between the stars. He envied them.

"Candidate Picard?" the young man said from his desk. "You may go in now."

"Thank you."

Counselor Trevalion was standing at his window, looking down at the same pond. "They are rather like starships," he said. "Each one self-contained and completely at home in its element."

Jean-Luc could not stop himself from thinking, *So he's a full telepath.*

Trevalion smiled at him. "I am," he said. "However, I cannot communicate directly to you mind-to-mind. I'm not quite that good. And you probably are more at ease speaking to me rather than just thinking through a conversation, so we'll keep things vocal for your comfort."

"Thank you," Jean-Luc said.

Trevalion tilted his head. "You are troubled."

Jean-Luc fought to keep all of his problems out of his mind: the blowup with his father, his worries about his future. It was useless. Like most people, Jean-Luc could not easily control his thoughts. If someone told him his life depended on his not thinking of a pink-striped zebra playing a tuba, he would have been a dead duck.

"I shall not pry into your personal affairs," Trevalion said. He smiled. "I'm afraid you will have to accept my word for that, but it is true. Please sit down, Mr. Picard."

Jean-Luc slipped into a comfortable seat beside Trevalion's desk, but he sat right on the edge. "I don't understand why I've been called here," he said.

Trevalion turned away from the window and stood against it, his hands behind his back. "Mmm. Tell me, Mr. Picard, what alternative plans did you have in mind?"

Jean-Luc blinked. "Alternative plans? What do you mean?"

"Well, after failing this test period. Surely you realized there was a possibility that you would not go to Starfleet Academy. After all, you already failed once."

Within him Jean-Luc's heart plummeted. So that was it. Something had gone wrong, and he had failed again. "I don't understand," he said, keeping his voice low.

"It's a simple question, really." Trevalion sounded concerned and friendly, but somehow distant, too, as if he were friendly only on a professional level. "Most of the other candidates have alternative plans. Many will become apprentices to the merchant services. Some will attend college or university here on Earth or within the system. One has received a provisional acceptance to the Vulcan Academy, a rare honor, indeed. But I find in your file no alternative plans at all. What will you do instead of going to Starfleet Academy?"

Jean-Luc looked at the floor. "I don't know."

"Well," Trevalion said, still in that cool, friendly voice, "perhaps I could suggest a few things to consider. You have your planet-side flying license. It wouldn't take much to upgrade you to a class two pilot's license that would be good for intersystem flying. Copernicus University on Luna has an excellent program for training independent pilots and technicians."

"No," Jean-Luc croaked. After a strained moment he added, "Thank you."

Silence hung heavy in the room. After a few moments Counselor Trevalion said softly, "I must point out, Mr. Picard, that your scores have been consistently very high. You have come in first or second in virtually every test. It would be a mistake for you to throw away your abilities by not attending college. If you want something more exotic, I might recommend the provincial institutions of Centauri System, or perhaps Barnard's System Omniversity—"

"Thank you, no," Jean-Luc said with more conviction. He stood. "May I go now?"

"No," Counselor Trevalion said. "You may not. You are in a highly disturbed emotional state. It is my job to help you deal with that. In my opinion, you can come

to terms with your anger and disappointment only by
making plans for the future.''

Jean-Luc's heart thudded heavily in his chest. He felt
light-headed, angry at himself and the world. When he
spoke, though, he tried hard to force all these feelings
back, to keep his voice level and even. "Thank you,
Counselor Trevalion. My plans are already made.''

"And what are they?"

With a bitter smile Jean-Luc said, "I am going to Starfleet Academy.''

When Counselor Trevalion gave his sympathetic smile
and a little shake of his head, Jean-Luc continued, "Oh,
I may not be going to fall term. And it may take me a
year or five years to get there, but I am going to Starfleet
Academy. In the meantime, I'll do whatever it takes to

earn my way there. I'll study, I'll work, I'll train myself. There are six testing cycles every year. Fine. Before I leave today, I'll sign up for the next testing cycle in the fall. And if I fail then, I'll sign up for the next one, and the one after that, until finally I pass."

"Is it failure that is so difficult for you to accept?" Trevalion asked.

"Yes. I was not raised to be a failure." Jean-Luc tugged his tunic self-consciously. "My father and mother taught me to persevere. And I suppose I inherited a certain amount of stubbornness, too."

"Will you be able to deal with yet another failure?" asked Trevalion. "I sense that you are very close to despair now."

He was right, but even so, Jean-Luc almost laughed. "I'll deal with anything that happens," he promised the counselor. "Good, bad, or indifferent. I will want copies of my test records, by the way."

"Surely, but why?"

"Because I can learn from my failures," Jean-Luc said. "I may not succeed next time, either, but I will not fail in the same way. I can promise you that."

The counselor appeared to think this over. "Very well," he said at last. "I wish you would make alternative plans, but if you're set on this course of action, I cannot prevent you. I will have the records transmitted to you. Where do you live?"

Jean-Luc swallowed. "There is some question about that," he said. "I'll be in touch."

"What makes you think you will be able to overcome

this"—Trevalion paused, as if groping for the right word—"this natural tendency toward failure?"

After taking a deep breath, Jean-Luc said, "I have a friend named Louis. He loves the sea. He's also terrified of it because he can't swim. But because his dream is larger than his fear, he begins studying on Medlab-One this autumn. Then there's my brother, Robert. He's afraid that my father cares more for me than for him— yet Robert was brave enough to wish me luck in my tests. If they can overcome their fears, then so can I."

"You are calmer now."

Jean-Luc blinked. Trevalion was right. He was calmer. The anger and resentment had faded away, replaced by a hot determination that, come what may, he would eventually be a Starfleet cadet. "I will be fine," he said. "May I go now?"

"In a moment." Trevalion picked up his data padd, made an entry on it, and then smiled at Jean-Luc. "Congratulations on passing the psych test," he said.

For a moment the counselor's words didn't register with Jean-Luc. Then he said, incredulously, "All this was a test?"

"The most difficult one, perhaps. I am sorry for the very real pain I caused you, Mr. Picard. You see, the psychology test forces a candidate to deal with whatever he or she dreads the most. In your case, that is failure. It is your one most deep-seated fear, the one part of yourself that you have the most difficulty confronting. You have taken your disappointment and anger and have directed them toward a new goal. It would have been easy for you to give in to despair, but you did not. Therefore, you have passed the psychology test."

Jean-Luc had a strange and empty sensation. "I don't know how to feel now," he said. "What does this mean?"

"You will know in about a week," Trevalion said. "You have done exceptionally well, but twelve others have done about the same. It will require further evaluation before the final decision is made. However, if you are not selected this time—"

"I will be back," Jean-Luc said, knowing it was true.

CHAPTER

10

The vineyard no longer seemed like home. Yvette had told Jean-Luc to come back, that Maurice was already sorry for his harsh words, but father and son hardly spoke anymore. When Maurice and Robert went to the vineyard each morning to work, Jean-Luc remained behind. He ran for scores of kilometers, just to work off his nervous energy. He read, tinkered with model starships, lifted weights. Nothing helped, not even a few sessions on the holophone with Louis, who had taken a nasty fall from his cycle and had shattered his left knee badly.

"It can be mended," Louis had said from his hospital bed, "but I'll be lame for two or three weeks." He sighed. "At least I have the lovely Bloom sisters as nurses. They are both most charmingly concerned about my poor leg."

"I think you did it on purpose," Jean-Luc teased. "You couldn't get them to fall in love with you for your personality, so now you're trying to win their sympathy."

"It might be worthwhile at that," responded Louis with a cheerful grin. "All's fair in love and cycling!"

Days passed. Before long it would be August. Starfleet Academy's fall term traditionally began the last week of August.

Jean-Luc moped. One morning his mother found him huddled at the top of the stair, reading a genuine, old-fashioned book. "You'll ruin your eyes," she said in mock horror.

"I always used to read here when I was little," Jean-Luc said. "It's so quiet and cool here on the stairway. I remember looking at a picture book of the planets here, and then later reading *The Three Musketeers* in this same spot. And now—" he broke off and shrugged.

Yvette sat beside him. "And now it doesn't seem the same."

"No." Jean-Luc smiled. "Are you part Betazoid? You can read my mind."

"I'm better than a Betazoid. I'm your mother," Yvette said. She sighed. "Robert has canceled his trip."

Jean-Luc nodded. "Yes, I know. He hasn't said anything, but the way he looks at me makes me feel terrible." He put his book down on his knee, open to his place. "Mother, I've been thinking. If I don't make it into the Academy this term, I'm applying to colleges on the western coast of North America. I may as well be close to the Academy for my next testing period."

"Very well," she said.

"I don't feel right, just staying here at home and not doing anything."

Yvette waited.

Finally Jean-Luc took a deep breath and admitted, "All right. I know that Father and Robert will grow closer without me around. Father still thinks he can talk me into being a winegrower. He's wrong, but he still thinks about it."

"Are you part Betazoid?"

With a rueful grin Jean-Luc said, "I'm better than a Betazoid. I'm his son." After another moment he added, "Perhaps we will both be happier if we're apart. Is that possible?"

Yvette put her arm around him. "Of course it is. You two are like reflections in a mirror. Except that each of you sees in his reflection what he does not like about himself. Haven't you ever wondered if your father ever regretted spending his life here in the vineyard?"

"Does he?" asked Jean-Luc in surprise.

"Well—not always. But from time to time he wonders what his life would have been like if he had not listened to his father. He had ideas of traveling, too, when he was your age. He gave them up. Now it pains him to see you have the same feelings. I think he is a little envious of you, that you will do things he never did, see things he never saw. But stronger than that envy are his love for you and his pride in you."

Jean-Luc murmured. "A mirror. Yes, in it I can see

what I do not want to become: a man so in love with the past that he cannot live in the present or look to the future. Perhaps it will be better, after all, when I move away."

"But you will come back," Yvette said. "And then your father will boast about you and will make much of you, and no matter what you have accomplished in the meantime, you will tell him how much you miss life here, the simple life in LaBarre."

"Will I?" he asked.

"Depend on it," Yvette said. "You are his son."

The call came two days later. Yvette's urgent voice summoned Jean-Luc to the holophone in the office. Beside his father's cluttered desk, Jean-Luc looked into the face of Commander Luttrell. "Are you packed, Mr. Picard?" she asked with a smile.

"I can pack," Jean-Luc said. It was suddenly hard to breathe.

"Then I advise you to do so. You have been accepted for the autumn term at Starfleet Academy. Orientation period will begin three weeks from today. I will transmit your orders immediately following this call. Congratulations, Cadet Picard."

Cadet Picard.

It had a nice ring to it.

It was a cool morning in August, one of those unusually chilly mornings that told you summer was ending and fall was on its way in. Jean-Luc stood at the LaBarre landing platform, his suitcases in his hands. Starfleet

Academy would issue his uniforms. He was bringing only a few things from home.

He had said his goodbyes at Chateau Picard. He and Maurice had shaken hands before his father had impulsively pulled him close and hugged him. "Well," he said gruffly, "if you're intent on this foolishness, then show them how well a Picard can do. See that they don't forget you!"

"I'll try," Jean-Luc had promised. He turned to Robert and held out the Saint Christopher's medal. "Here," he said. "And thanks for lending it to me."

"It was a gift," Robert said with a grin. "You keep it, genius. You may still need a little luck now and then."

And Yvette had said almost nothing at all. She had simply embraced him and had whispered, "I love you, son."

He shivered. He had come out early, far too early, but he was too excited to stay in the skyport. The trouble was there was nothing to do out here, either, except to scan the clear morning sky for any sign of—

"There he is!" shouted a familiar voice.

Jean-Luc turned in surprise. Hurrying toward him was Louis, limping gamely along, with Kim Bloom at his right elbow and Misty Bloom at his left, both partly supporting him. "Sneak off, would you?" boomed Louis. "I should yank your hair out for that!"

"Not my hair!" yelped Jean-Luc in mock alarm.

"Easy," warned Misty as Louis lunged at Jean-Luc to deliver a playful punch.

"He's not a very good patient," Kim told Jean-Luc. "If he were a kangaroo, I'd sedate him."

"Well," Louis said, "so this is it."

"Yes," agreed Jean-Luc. "I want to thank you. You were an inspiration to me."

"Hear that, girls?" Louis roared, throwing an arm around both their shoulders. "And you thought I was so useless!"

Which one will he settle on? Jean-Luc wondered. Both Bloom girls were gazing at Louis with obvious fondness. *Oh, well,* he thought. *I may have my troubles at the Academy, but Louis is letting himself in for some real problems!* Aloud, he said, "Seriously, you're my best friend. You take care on the bottom of that ocean."

"And you out there in space," Louis returned. More quietly, he said, "Don't worry, Jean-Luc. I know your father. Maurice may be a gruff old bear, but by the time you come home for the holidays, he'll be bragging about you to anyone within hearing distance."

"It's nice of you to say so," Jean-Luc answered. Inside, though, he wasn't so sure. Only time could tell.

"Look!" Misty Bloom shouted. "Here it comes!"

Jean-Luc looked up into the sky. There, so far above them that it was merely a hurtling silvery speck, was the descending shuttle. In moments it would set down, Jean-Luc would board it, and he would step into the joys and the sorrows, the failures and the successes, of his future.

It frightened him a little. For all its worries, his past had been comfortable, known, reliable. But the future— well, the future was vast and unknown, and it stretched ahead for long, long years.

Jean-Luc straightened his shoulders and smiled in anticipation. Whatever that future might hold, he would live it among the stars.

About the Authors

BRAD AND BARBARA STRICKLAND are a husband-and-wife writing team from Oakwood, Georgia. Brad has written or co-written eighteen novels and more than sixty short stories, including two *Star Trek: Deep Space Nine* novels for young readers, *The Star Ghost* and *Stowaways*. Barbara makes her writing debut as co-author of the two *Starfleet Academy* novels *Starfall* and *Nova Command*. Together they are writing three novels for the Nickelodeon *Are You Afraid of the Dark?* series, also available from Minstrel Books.

Both Stricklands are teachers. Brad is an Associate Professor of English at Gainesville College, and Barbara teaches second grade at Myers Elementary School. They have a son, Jonathan, a daughter, Amy, and numerous pets. In addition to writing, Brad likes travel, sailing, and photography, and Barbara is a great *Star Trek* fan and enjoys crafts. She won first prize for children's costumes at the World Science Fiction Convention in Atlanta, GA. Both husband and wife know how to bathe a ferret.

About the Illustrator

TODD CAMERON HAMILTON is a self-taught artist who has resided all his life in Chicago, Illinois. He has been a professional illustrator for the past ten years, specializing in fantasy, science fiction, and horror. Todd is the current president of the Association of Science Fiction and Fantasy Artists. His original works grace many private and corporate collections. He has co-authored two novels and several short stories. When not drawing, painting, or writing, his interests include metalsmithing, puppetry, and teaching.

Beam aboard for new adventures!

A new title every other month!

Pocket Books presents a new, illustrated series for younger readers based on the hit television show STAR TREK: DEEP SPACE NINE®.

Young Jake Sisko is looking for friends aboard the space station. He finds Nog, a Ferengi his own age, and together they find a whole lot of trouble!

#1: THE STAR GHOST
#2: STOWAWAYS
by Brad Strickland

#3: PRISONERS OF PEACE
by John Peel

#4: THE PET
by Mel Gilden and Ted Pedersen

#5: ARCADE
by Diana G. Gallagher

#6: FIELD TRIP
by John Peel

Published by Pocket Books

954-04